HAUNTED
GRAVEYARD
OF THE PACIFIC

D1572254

HAUNTED
GRAVEYARD
OF THE PACIFIC

IRA WESLEY KITMACHER

Haunted
America

Published by Haunted America
A Division of The History Press
Charleston, SC
www.historypress.com

Copyright © 2021 by Ira Wesley Kitmacher
All rights reserved

Photograph of North Head Lighthouse grounds, Ilwaco, Washington. *Author's collection*.
Pacific Northwest forest highway. *Courtesy of Pixabay*.
Photograph of the wrecked *Peter Iredale*, Hammond, Oregon, 2014. *Courtesy of 9thstreetdesign, Pixabay*.

First published 2021

Manufactured in the United States

ISBN 9781467149501

Library of Congress Control Number: 2021937165

Notice: The information in this book is true and complete to the best of our knowledge. It is offered without guarantee on the part of the author or The History Press. The author and The History Press disclaim all liability in connection with the use of this book.

All rights reserved. No part of this book may be reproduced or transmitted in any form whatsoever without prior written permission from the publisher except in the case of brief quotations embodied in critical articles and reviews.

I dedicate this book to my beloved family.

—*Ira Wesley Kitmacher*

CONTENTS

CONTENTS

INTRODUCTION

WHY I WROTE THIS BOOK

As a fairly new resident of the Pacific Northwest—the Astoria, Oregon area to be exact—I'm fascinated by the area's history and culture. The Pacific Northwest was one of the last parts of the United States to be explored and settled, making it seem more "wild" than other parts of the country.

Astoria is a rustic, beautiful Victorian coastal city that was established in 1811. It is the oldest permanent American settlement west of the Rocky Mountains and is often referred to as "the San Francisco of the Northwest" due to its hilly topography and architecture. South of Astoria, there are many lovely and scenic coastal towns, while the major city of Portland, Oregon, lies just inland and serves as our starting point. North of Astoria is Washington State's Long Beach Peninsula, nicknamed the "Cape Cod of the Pacific," due, in part, to its twenty-eight-mile-long flat sandy beach. Some say visiting Long Beach is like "stepping back in time," to a simpler, quainter period. North of the Long Beach Peninsula is the wild Washington Coast, bordered by towering fir and spruce trees, as well as vast redcedar and redwood forests. The lovely city of Victoria, British Columbia (BC), Canada, lies just north of the border, while the largest city on our road trip, Seattle, Washington, serves as our end point.

Rustic seaside villages, lighthouses, restaurants, antique stores, surf shops and carnivals abound, while farmer's markets and weekly tourist festivals

Photograph of the Astoria, Oregon waterfront, 1860–1920. *Courtesy of the Miriam and Ira D. Wallach Photography Collection, New York Public Library.*

welcome residents and visitors alike. The area is known for great boating, camping, fishing, biking, clamming, golfing, cranberry cultivation, oyster farming and tourism activities, while state parks with nineteenth-century military forts and national historic sites welcome history enthusiasts. Bald eagles, black bears, elk, deer and other wildlife call the area home, and gray whales can be spotted migrating twice a year.

Despite this idyllic setting, there is another, darker name by which the area is known: the Graveyard of the Pacific. More than two thousand ships and countless lives have been lost to the treacherous waters of the Pacific Ocean and Columbia River. The combination of river flow and offshore currents create an ever-shifting hazardous sand bar at the mouth of the 1,214-mile-long Columbia River (one of the longest rivers in the United States), and unlike other rivers, whose power dissipates as it drains into deltas, the Columbia River funnels water like a powerful fire hose into the Pacific Ocean. This, together with frequent thick fog and violent storms from the North Pacific have caused ships to sink, burn and be crushed against the shore. Mariners and passengers have been swallowed by the waters for

Artist's rendering of a shipwreck victim, 1913. *Courtesy of the Miriam and Ira D. Wallach Photography Collection, New York Public Library.*

as long as can be remembered. The spirits of sailors and passengers who suffered these dramatic shipwrecks are said to linger.

As humans, we have particularly short memories. We remember what just happened and what happened a few days or weeks ago. But few seem to remember what happened years—let alone a century—ago. This is true of disasters as well. We remember the airline accident that happened a year ago, as it is still in the news, yet we have virtually no memory of long-ago shipwrecks (other than that of the *Titanic* and a few others) that resulted in multiple deaths. These disasters were all too common in the days before satellite navigation, GPS and cellphones.

The Graveyard of the Pacific's reportedly high level of paranormal activity is not limited to the sea. On land, the spirits of sailors who were "shanghaied" for involuntary service onboard ships, women who were kidnapped for prostitution and slavery and lighthouse keepers and their families who suffered tragic deaths are said to linger. Other lingering spirits are said to include those of early settlers, perhaps wishing to remain close to their homes and descendants or to complete unfinished business, Natives whose lands were stolen and burial grounds desecrated, murderers and murder victims and soldiers. In addition to these ghost stories, there are countless supernatural tales of Sasquatch, werewolves and legends of buried treasure.

Chilling tales of paranormal occurrences abound in this northwestern corner of America. It's no wonder that movies and television shows like the vampire and werewolf movie series *The Twilight Saga*, the pirate treasure movie *The Goonies*, the tv series *Supernatural*, the remake of *The Fog* and the drama-mystery *Twin Peaks* were either made or based in the region. Even the movie *The Shining* featured a package of "Willapoint Minced Clams," which are sourced along the Graveyard of the Pacific.

The dark skies, wind, storms and fog all add to an atmosphere of mystery and dread. Damaging storms frequently strike the Pacific Northwest, devastating whole towns. The area is at risk from tsunamis, giant ocean waves caused by earthquakes; the last major tsunami struck the area in 1700 and was so powerful it swallowed entire Native villages. Reflecting this foreboding atmosphere, local landmarks are colorfully named "Cape Disappointment"

Photograph of Merriweather Lewis, 2007. *Courtesy of Photoman, Pixabay.*

(a ship's captain was disappointed to not find the Columbia River), "Deadman's Hollow" (where victims of a shipwreck washed ashore) and "Dismal Nitch" (where Lewis and Clark took shelter during a fierce 1805 winter storm while exploring the Northwest).

So, if you see someone on land who appears out of place or hear ghostly words on the wind, check again—it may be the forlorn spirit of a lost soul reaching out.

My Beliefs and Approach

Those who believe in ghosts and supernatural phenomenon say restless spirits haunt the area, while others point to the tales of Natives and early settlers. We will explore many of these tales and legends.

I would not describe myself as a "full believer" of these stories, though I find them fascinating and would like to believe that some—or at least part—of the legends are true. When I travel, I like to dig into the history of the area, which often includes participating in "ghost tours." I've done this in Charleston, South Carolina; Gettysburg, Pennsylvania; Salem Massachusetts; Tombstone, Arizona; Williamsburg, Virginia; and other historic towns. These towns are said to be haunted by Civil War soldiers, gunfighters, colonial residents and others. As a professor, attorney and former senior executive, it is my nature to question whether these tales are based on fact and logic. But in researching these tales, it is clear that not everything can be proven beyond a reasonable doubt.

I use an evidence-based approach in analyzing these reported supernatural phenomena. I have not included legends and stories that lack any evidence.

Legends and tales of hauntings may serve many purposes. For believers, these tales may simply document paranormal activity. For others, they may help explain that which is not easily explained. For others still, much like the experience of telling ghost stories around a fire, such tales can be a fun escape from reality. Whatever the reason, these tales are fascinating and are part of an area's history.

I view my role as multifaceted: historian, investigator, interested taleteller, prideful resident and tour guide. It is through these lenses that I write this book. I have conducted significant research and have included it as it is applicable (please see the bibliography). The amount of evidence I was able to identify varies from tale to tale, and I have included what I could find. In some cases, based on the tale, I have added (and identified) my own speculation. I hope you enjoy reading it as much as I enjoyed writing it!

Please join me as we take a road trip through this fascinating—and, arguably, most haunted—place in America!

PART I

THE MOST HAUNTED PLACE IN AMERICA: THE GRAVEYARD OF THE PACIFIC

1
GHOSTS AND OTHER UNDEAD

As highlighted in a 2017 *USA Today* article, 45 percent of people surveyed believe in ghosts, 32 percent believe ghosts can hurt the living and 18 percent reported having been in the presence of a ghost. This belief in ghosts has existed for as long as humans have inhabited the Earth. Tales of ghosts were present in ancient Egypt, Mesopotamia, ancient Greece, the Roman Empire, Native American and Aboriginal cultures and across many religions.

The scientific view is that ghosts and supernatural phenomenon are simply the products of optical illusions, hallucinations or other explainable maladies or logical errors.

For believers, ghosts and supernatural phenomenon can be good, evil or something in between. They may represent an omen or portent of death, or they may not. Ghosts are often thought of as spirits that have not "passed on" but rather are trapped or connected to earthly property, memories, the living or some unfinished business. Often, but not always, the deceased met a sudden, unexpected death, such as an accident or a violent or tragic death.

The word *ghost* comes from Old English and refers to the human spirit or soul of the deceased. I use several different words interchangeably within this book, including ghost, apparition, haunt, phantom, poltergeist, specter and spirit. Different cultures have different ideas about ghosts, although most have some belief in an afterlife.

Ghosts generally take on one of five forms:

- ECTOPLASM OR ECTO-MIST: A vaporous cloud, floating above the ground, white, gray or black. They have been witnessed in graveyards, battlefields and historical sites, among other places.

- FUNNELS: Frequently experienced in homes or historical buildings as cold spots, wisps or swirling spirals of light. Many of us have experienced cold spots and wondered if it's an air circulation issue or perhaps something more sinister.

- INANIMATE OBJECTS: Including ghost ships, ghost trains and other vehicles believed to be controlled by the undead who were involved in accidents, wrecks or suffering other sudden and unexpected ends. Examples include the old City of Albany ghost train, featured in 1989's Ghostbusters II (really an amalgam of multiple train wrecks), which was said to have killed over one hundred people after it derailed in 1920; and the Flying Dutchman, a legendary ghost ship most likely based on seventeenth-century Dutch East India Company ships, which is said to be doomed to sail forever.

- INTERACTIVE PERSONALITY: Of a known deceased person, a family member, historical figure or someone else. The entity can make itself visible, speak, make noise and let you know it is present. It may be visiting to comfort the living or perhaps because it believes the living want to see them. An example is British prime minister Winston Churchill seeing the spirit of America's sixteenth president, Abraham Lincoln, in 1944 at the White House. Churchill had just stepped out of the bath and reportedly said, "Good evening, Mr. President, you seem to have me at a disadvantage."

- ORBS: Appear as a transparent or translucent hovering ball of light. Sometimes, they go unnoticed until a photograph or video is later viewed. These entities are often seen in television ghost hunter programs.

- POLTERGEIST: German for "noisy ghost," a poltergeist is thought to be able to move or knock things over, make noise, manipulate the physical environment, turn lights on and off, slam doors and even start fires. They are often depicted as dangerous, as seen in the 1982 Steven Spielberg horror movie *Poltergeist*.

As we know from books and movies, the undead can take on forms other than ghosts. These are often portrayed as dangerous, evil, vengeful creatures that prey on the living. We'll talk about several on our road trip, including:

- monsters (mythical creatures, such as the Kraken sea monster);
- mummies (an intentionally preserved corpse);
- vampires (feed on the blood of humans and other living beings);
- werewolves (people who transform into large wolf-like creatures); and
- zombies (reanimated corpses that feed on flesh).

2

SEAFARING SUPERSTITIONS

The area we will be exploring—and its reported paranormal activity—is heavily influenced by seafaring legacies and accompanying superstitions. One nineteenth-century fatalistic belief among sailors was: "What the sea wants, the sea will have." This was because many sailors could not swim, and even bathing in the ocean was considered dangerous. In the seafaring realm, it's considered unlucky to begin a voyage on a Friday because Jesus was crucified on a Friday. Seeing a person with red hair, who is cross-eyed or flat-footed was thought to be bad luck. Flowers, ministers and ringing bells are thought to be for funerals and, thus, forecast death and bad luck. If someone's sweetheart brought flowers onboard, the flowers were thrown overboard. The crew's intentional ringing of the ship's bells was exempted from the superstition, but if the bells rang on their own—even by the wind, without human cause—it was thought to be a sign that someone was going to die. Killing a dolphin, a gull or an albatross brought bad luck, as did stepping aboard with your left foot, losing a bucket overboard or seeing rats running off the ship.

The old adage "Red sky in the morning, sailors take warning. Red sky at night, sailors' delight," is thought to have some basis in fact. If the air is clear, sunset is said to be tinted red. But red light in the morning may mean moisture is in the air, thus increasing the likelihood of stormy weather. Clapping hands aboard a ship and the presence of umbrellas were thought to tempt thunder and foul weather. Throwing stones into the ocean was thought to cause storms and huge swells. Strange sounds heard while at sea were often blamed on sirens or mermaids whose songs could lure sailors to their deaths. The sight of a bare-breasted woman was thought to calm an angry sea, hence ships' figureheads often being bare breasted, well-endowed women. A ship's name ending in the letter "a" was considered unlucky, and some would say the *Lusitania* and the *Britannia* proved this point when they were sunk by German torpedoes.

Other seafaring superstitions include never painting your ship green, as doing so will cause the vessel to beach itself in a gale. Turning a cup or bucket upside down will cause the boat to overturn. Whistling in the wheelhouse will cause high winds. Always batten down the hatches and never leave a hatch cover laying upside down. When heading to the ship, one should never turn back, and saying the word *pig* was to be avoided at all costs. Many at-sea calamities are said to be linked to the violation of these superstitions.

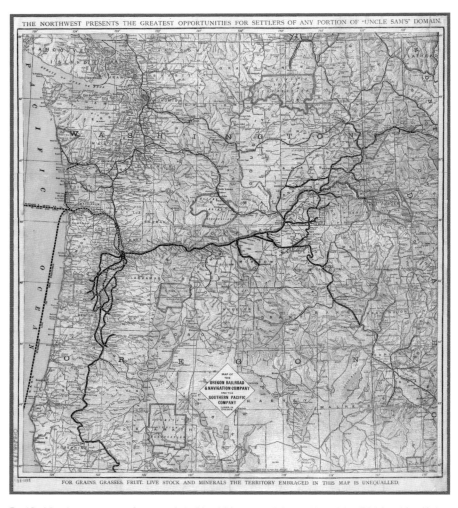

Pacific Northwest, 1898. *Courtesy of the Lionel Pincus and Princess Firyal Map Division, New York Public Library.*

PART II.

HAUNTED ROAD TRIP ON LAND AND SEA (SOUTH TO NORTH)

1

PORTLAND, OREGON

HAUNTINGS GALORE

Portland, Oregon, is the first stop and entryway to our road trip through the Graveyard of the Pacific. Portland is the second-largest city (after Seattle) we will explore and is said to be one of the most haunted places in America. Sitting at the junction of the Columbia and Willamette Rivers, in the shadow of Mount Hood, Portland is nicknamed the "Rose City" and is blessed with both natural beauty and culture, though it may also be home to a number of haunted locations and personalities.

Like much of the Pacific Northwest, Lewis and Clark's Corps of Discovery scouted the Oregon Country (as the region was known in the nineteenth century) in 1805 on behalf of President Thomas Jefferson. Interest in the region grew after the corps reported on the mild climate, fertile land, green forests and many lakes and rivers located in the Pacific Northwest. In 1843, William Overton of Tennessee and his friend Massachusetts lawyer Asa Lovejoy floated down the Willamette River and discovered the area that would become Portland. Soon after they started to clear the land, Overton sold his share to Francis Pettygrove of Maine. In 1845, Lovejoy and Pettygrove flipped a coin to decide on a name for the city. Pettygrove won and named the city after Portland, Maine. Portland grew quickly, especially after the Civil War, becoming a major port and shipping center.

D 71 PANORAMA OF PORTLAND, OREGON. (No. 1.)

Photograph of Portland, Oregon, 1880–89. *Courtesy of the Miriam and Ira D. Wallach Photography Collection, New York Public Library.*

SPECTRAL SHANGHAI TUNNELS

Beneath Portland's Old Town Chinatown—the original downtown—snake shanghai tunnels. Although not completely clear, the tunnels received their name either based on the fact that they were built under Chinatown by Chinese workers or because China was the destination for many kidnapped sailors. Countless men were illegally kidnapped (or "crimped") to serve unwillingly aboard ships. The word *crimp* has two potential origins. The first comes from British slang for "agent" and refers to a tactic used by the Royal Navy to "impress" or force sailors into serving aboard ships. The other comes from the Dutch word *krimp*, meaning "a holding tank for live fish." These tunnels ran from downtown bars and hotels to the waterfront along the Willamette River, and sailors were led through them to serve unwillingly on ships in need of crews. These men were drugged or knocked unconscious, waking up to find themselves aboard ships and out at sea. Women were likewise kidnapped and led to underground brothels, forced into prostitution or slavery. Opium dens, gambling houses and prisons were also said to be within the tunnels. The 2020 Travel Channel program *Portals to Hell* explored the tunnels.

The most infamous shanghaier (and opium smuggler) was Bunko (sometimes spelled "Bunco") Kelly. He was a British hotelier who, by his own account, crimped some two thousand men and women over a fifteen-year period, beginning in 1879. He earned his nickname "Bunko" in 1887 after delivering a crimped "cripple" to the captain of the British ship *Jupiter*. The captain complained Kelly's action was "bunk," or ridiculous. As shanghaiing wasn't illegal at the time, Kelly was never arrested for it. However, he was arrested and convicted of murder in 1895 for the killing of G.W. Sayres, an opium smuggler who was hacked to death and thrown into the Willamette River.

Kelly was sent to the Oregon State Penitentiary, which was built in 1851, making it the oldest prison in the state. He wrote about his experiences in prison, including his observations of prisoners killing guards, brutality, floggings (later replaced with spraying prisoners with cold water), negligent doctors and other abuses in his book *Thirteen Years in Oregon State Penitentiary*. He was pardoned by the governor in 1908, based on a petition filed by some of the same people who had worked to have him incarcerated.

Kelly's most infamous crimping reportedly took place in 1893. He was looking for seventeen men to kidnap and provide to a ship headed to Shanghai. He passed a Portland funeral home and heard multiple men groaning. Kelly found twenty-two seemingly drunken men in the cellar and a keg of deadly embalming fluid from which they had been drinking. He had his men load the twenty-two dying men into carts, then canoes and finally delivered them to the ship's captain. The captain paid Kelly, only to later discover the twenty-two sailors dead in the ship's hold. The captain had to secure seventeen additional sailors when he reached Astoria. No investigation was ever conducted.

Artist's rendering of Bunko Kelly. *Courtesy of the* Portland Evening Telegram, *1894.*

Tales have been told for well over a century of the shanghai tunnels being haunted by the victims of these crimes, as well as the criminals themselves. In their Victorian heyday in the late 1800s, Portland's waterfront neighborhoods were considered the seedier side of the city, home to saloons, brothels and boardinghouses that catered to sailors. Portland was considered one of the most dangerous cities in the world; its other nickname was the "Forbidden City."

Young men out for a night of drinking at saloons such as Erickson's, the Snug Harbor and the Valhalla would sometimes wake the next morning, shocked to find they were on board a ship headed for Asia or another foreign location. They had been shanghaied. They were dropped through trapdoors or carried unconscious through underground tunnels to waiting ships, where they were sold as slave labor for fifty dollars a head. There was no escape.

It is on the waterfront and in these tunnels that supernatural activity is said to abound. The apparitions of the undead linger in these musty, wet, abandoned and underground locations. Portland has more than its fair share of paranormal legends.

One such legend surrounds the untimely deaths of the shanghaied crewmembers aboard the *Jennifer Jo*. These sailors were beaten, starved and drugged before being dragged, unconscious, to the ship. The ship departed the Portland dock at night, only to sink soon after in the Columbia River. The shanghaied crew members were held prisoner below the decks, and that is where they drowned. Visitors to the tunnels have reported being touched by wet hands; hearing disembodied screaming, moaning and murmuring voices, footsteps, heavy breathing; and having heavy, uneasy feelings. These are said to be the ghosts of the *Jennifer Jo*'s crew, lingering as a result of their sudden, violent deaths, or perhaps because they feel that they have unfinished business in the land of the living.

BENSON HOTEL POLTERGEISTS

Built in 1913, the Benson Hotel is a twelve-story, 287 room, luxurious landmark hotel located in downtown Portland. In 2014, *USA Today* identified the Benson Hotel as one of the most haunted hotels in the world.

The Benson Hotel is said to be haunted by its former owner, namesake and pioneer lumberman Simon Benson, who died in 1942. His spirit is said to be present, dressed in a formal dark suitcoat. Simon, as someone who never drank alcohol, was known as a "teetotaler." In life, he discouraged his workers from drinking alcohol. He also donated $10,000 to the city of Portland to install twenty bronze drinking fountains, called "Benson Bubblers," to provide people with something to drink other than alcohol. Benson's spirit has been blamed for disapprovingly knocking over patrons' drinks. His ghost has been seen "floating" down the staircase, checking in on

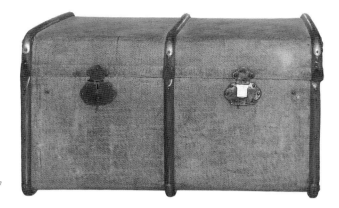

Photograph of an old travel chest, 2018. *Courtesy of Anaterate, Pixabay.*

service and standing at the back of a conference room, listening as a meeting began. This was his dream hotel, and it is believed he doesn't want to leave.

Other ghosts witnessed at the Benson Hotel include a three-year-old brown-haired boy who reportedly appeared at a female guest's bedside. She was the mother of her own three-year-old and felt a maternal instinct toward the spirit. They interacted, with the woman touching the ghost's arm, which she reported felt real. The spirit made a funny, scary face. This interaction continued for several minutes until the little boy disappeared. The next morning, the woman asked while checking out and found that other guests had similarly seen the little boy.

An unknown female, middle-aged ghost wearing a turquoise dress and red rings on her fingers has been seen as a reflection in the lobby mirror, looking back at the guests. Another woman dressed in white has been reported roaming the halls.

There is another male spirit, appearing to be a hotel porter, who is said to have gently assisted a disabled guest into bed, then disappeared. This spirit has been reported by other guests, assisting them in similar ways.

Finally, there have been reports of disembodied ballroom music, voices and shadow figures within the hotel.

WHITE EAGLE SALOON AND HOTEL PHANTOMS

A saloon—originally the B. Soboleski & Company Saloon—has stood at this site since at least the 1850s. The formerly rough waterfront saloon was once the scene of violent brawls and was nicknamed the "Bucket of Blood."

Dock workers and sailors frequented the saloon. The White Eagle Saloon and Hotel is a historic, two-story brick fixture, which some say is haunted. Several apparitions are said to reside here: a prostitute named Rose, an aggressive bouncer, a bartender and the souls of unwitting victims who were kidnapped via the nearby shanghai tunnels.

One of the bar's spirits is that of Sam Warrick, a pre-Prohibition, hard-drinking bartender, cook and handyman who rented a room in the hotel for forty years and stayed there until his death. Warrick's photograph is part of the hotel's historic photograph collection, and his ghost has been seen throwing condiments across the kitchen. He is also said to back up toilets in the downstairs bathroom, even when the saloon is closed.

Both the second floor and the basement were once used for prostitution. Reflecting the prejudice of the time, the Black, Asian and Latino prostitutes, said to have been kidnapped or enslaved, worked out of the basement, while their White counterparts worked from the upper floor. The basement was also an opium den. Rose is said to have been a "working girl" on the second floor for many years. The tale is that Rose fell in love with a sailor who also loved her but was married. The sailor left on a voyage, and when he returned, he found that Rose had been murdered. The murderer is said to have been a spurned lover of Rose who had proposed marriage, but Rose declined out of fear of reprisal by her boss. Rose is said to haunt the upstairs rooms of the hotel, with witnesses reporting seeing her spirit looking out the upper-floor window of the room in which she was murdered. Witnesses also report hearing a woman moaning, sobbing and weeping, like she is waiting for her lover to return. The rooms of the upper floor have been closed and unoccupied since the 1950s. In the basement, doors open and shut on their own, faint dance hall music and disembodied voices can be heard, witnesses have felt cold hands touching them, objects have moved on their own and coins have been seen inexplicably falling out of the air.

A bouncer, described as "scary and menacing," who worked at the saloon in the early twentieth century before disappearing without a trace, is also said to haunt the building. In one case, his spirit is credited with throwing a large white board off a wall and down the stairs after an employee walked past it. In another case, an employee was struck with a basement freezer door that opened and closed on its own several times. The employee refused to go down to the basement again.

Ghostly Edgefield Hotel

The 1911 McMenamin's Edgefield Hotel is a luxurious destination and resort, but it formerly served as a "poorhouse for the deplorable," the sick, poor and homeless. Many of its former residents, either too old or feeble to leave, lived at the facility until after World War II. Many of these residents died in the building due to old age, illness and epidemics—and their spirits are said to still linger.

One spirit is said to be the mother of a newborn who died from chicken pox. The mother and baby were reportedly buried on the property, and the mother has been heard on the upper floors calming her crying baby. She is described as singing soothing nursery rhymes.

An employee of three and a half years reported seeing a nurse in the upstairs hallway, formerly the poorhouse infirmary. The spirit was wearing a nurse's hat and pantyhose and was carrying keys and a bucket. She turned toward the employee and vanished. The same employee reported feeling an energy pass "right through [her] chest" as she walked down the hallway. Another employee told of someone dropping something above them and it rolling down the rafters, even though no guests or staff were in the rafters above.

Another less friendly spirit is said to have haunted a female guest's room, telling the manager to "get out" when he was called to investigate. Others have reported feeling spirits "pushing" them, hearing disembodied whispers and seeing the spirit of an elderly woman who taps guests on the shoulder and throws their clothing around the room.

Old Town Pizza Spirits

Old Town Pizza, known for great pizza and a fun atmosphere, was formerly the Old Town Merchant Hotel, dating back to the 1800s. Legend has it that a "working woman" named Nina was killed there, and her spirit still lingers. Nina is said to have worked as a prostitute to support her twelve-year-old daughter. The basement of the Merchant Hotel served as a brothel, and Nina cooperated with missionaries who wished to close the brothel and "clean up the neighborhood." In exchange, they promised to "free" Nina from her difficult life and help her build a new one. She was later found dead, thrown down the elevator shaft. Her daughter soon disappeared, and no record of her whereabouts has ever been found. It is assumed an angry "john" or lover killed Nina.

Nina's spirit, described as sad and mournful, has reportedly been seen wandering through the former hotel lobby and basement, wearing a long black dress. Some witnesses say she taps them on the shoulder. Others report the scent of perfume, disembodied whispers and a child's laughter from behind the bar. A frightened delivery person said he saw a "body of smoke" floating by the basement stairs, which then "rushed up the stairs." A brick at the bottom of the elevator shaft bears Nina's name.

One female witness described going to Old Town Pizza's ladies' room, turning toward the vanity and seeing Nina's ghost. As she hastily exited, the witness glanced at the mirror and saw Nina standing behind her. The witness said she wasn't drunk or hallucinating. She described Nina as being pale with a slight blue hue to her complexion; she had long, black, straight hair and was wearing a long black dress.

KELL'S IRISH RESTAURANT + PUB APPARITION

Kell's Irish Restaurant & Pub is described as cool, with great food, and it is also said to be haunted by the ghost of longtime Portland fire chief David Campbell. According to Portland's Fire and Rescue Website, Campbell was a firefighter for thirty years and chief for fourteen starting in 1895. He was elected by his peers as the president of the Pacific Coast Fire Chiefs' Association in 1906. On June 26, 1911, an oil pump at the Union Oil Distributing Plant in Portland was set on fire. Chief Campbell, seeing that an internal attack on the fire was needed, borrowed a coat from one of his men and went into the building. Gases accumulated, an explosion occurred and bodies were thrown across the street as building materials were blown two hundred feet into the air. Campbell's body was recovered, huddled in his borrowed coat with the letters "F.D." still visible on the buttons. He was forty-seven years old. Campbell was well respected and seen as a major force in modernizing Portland's fire department. His funeral in 1911 drew more than 150,000 mourners.

Witnesses in Kell's Pub have seen Chief Campbell's ghost in his full firefighter gear in the pub's basement Cigar Room. He has been described as "friendly." A piano downstairs has also been observed playing itself. The Cigar Room is attached to what were once shanghai tunnels, and the sounds of disembodied heavy breathing, chairs being rearranged and televisions being turned on have been heard; sightings of a face in the mirror and other paranormal activities have also been reported.

HAUNTED HOLLYWOOD THEATER

The historic Hollywood Theater has been in operation since July 17, 1926, and is one of the oldest remaining theaters in the United States. One of the first advertisements for the theater described it as a "palace of luxury, comfort and entertainment unsurpassed by any theater on the coast." It is truly a majestic structure, which has been described by some as resembling an ornate, medieval church. In 1983, it was listed in the National Register of Historic Places.

Theatergoers and staff have reported weird sensations while in the theater. Witnesses have seen the ghost of a well-dressed middle-age man floating in the upstairs lobby. On investigating, the ghost identified himself (via an electronic "spirit box") as Steve, and for most of his life, he said he worked at the theater until he became sick and passed away. He loved the theater so much he didn't want to leave. A young blonde female spirit has been seen nervously pacing in high heels, smoking a cigarette in the upstairs theater. She appears to be waiting for someone to join her. She taps people on the shoulder then vanishes with a giggle when they turn to see her. Another male spirit taps people on the shoulder and whispers unintelligibly. There is said to be another female spirit sitting quietly in the back row of the theater.

A paranormal investigator, on exiting the women's restroom, reported feeling freezing cold and encountering a swirling spirit approaching her before vanishing. Witnesses have heard voices saying "Hey, you!" and have seen strange funnels, vortices, swirling lights and orbs that create cold spots.

LONELY LONE FIR CEMETERY

Lone Fir Cemetery is Portland's largest pioneer-era graveyard. Established in 1855, it serves as the final resting place for twenty-five thousand souls. Nearly ten thousand grave markers have been left illegible as a result of age and exposure to the elements. Due to a lack of records, no one knows who

Photograph of a cemetery, 2016. *Courtesy of Pixabay.*

the ten thousand markers belong to. A Soldier's Monument was built in 1903 that commemorates the area's dead in the Native, Mexican-American, Civil and Spanish-American Wars.

The Lone Fir Cemetery serves as the backdrop for numerous ghostly tales and legends. The story of Anne Jeanne Tingry-LeCoz, also known as Emma Merlotin, is perhaps the most well-known. Born in France in 1850, Merlotin (died 1885, age thirty-five) was reportedly a courtesan, "wayward girl," "fallen woman" or, as Portland's *Evening Telegram* phrased it, a "nymph du pave." She was said to have wealthy, upper-class and powerful clients. On December 22, 1885, a very cold and rainy night, Merlotin was brutally hacked to death with a hatchet at her home at Southeast Third and Yamhill Streets, in the "Tenderloin" District, also known as the "Court of Death." The area earned this nickname due to it being a "red-light district," experiencing prostitution, violence and multiple murders. The brutal murders of prostitutes occurred with increasing and alarming regularity in the 1880s.

A police officer heard her screams and found her just before 11:00 p.m., lying face down in a three-foot-wide pool of blood. Local newspapers described in graphic detail Merlotin clothed in only a chemise, boots and stockings. She suffered a gruesome bludgeoning and slashing, with twelve wounds to her head and arms. Merlotin's close friend Amelia told police she heard Emma greet and laugh with a male visitor, then scream just before her murder took place. Portland police first thought the motive was robbery, but they soon found a gold ring that had fallen off her finger on the floor nearby. She was also still wearing her gold earrings and had $15 on her person (about $500 today). A sailor, William Sundstrom, was arrested "prowling around" the murder scene and trying to enter Merlotin's cottage. He had a badly scratched face, which he claimed was due to his "falling against a tree trunk," bloody pants and a bloody hatchet at his house. Though he claimed the hatchet was covered in red paint, on examination, it was found to be blood. While police arrested Sundstrom, they did not charge him or anyone else with Merlotin's murder. There is no apparent reason for this other than, perhaps, a possible bias against prostitutes. Rumors also swirled that no one was charged because one of Merlotin's clients was a "crazy" member of a prominent Portland family.

Merlotin was buried in block 20, lot 18, 2S of Lone Fir Cemetery, and visitors have reported seeing a shadowy female figure dressed in nineteenth-century French fashion roaming the cemetery. When approached, the figure throws up her hands, screams and vanishes. As recently as May 8, 2019, flowers have been left anonymously at Merlotin's grave. Her murder has been the subject of several television programs. Because 1880s scientists believed the last thing a person saw before death was preserved in their eyes' retinas, as the *Oregonian* reported, one of Merlotin's eyes was removed and given to a well-known local photographer for later study.

According to the Metro Council (a regional government agency), thousands of bodies were buried in the cemetery's block 14, a 1.25-acre plot in a corner of the cemetery. These included the bodies of over two hundred deceased patients from the Oregon Hospital for the Insane (also known as the Hawthorne Asylum), which was established in 1862 and closed in 1883. Most of its records were destroyed in a fire in 1888. According to the Metro Council, these patients suffered from mental illness, had physical disabilities, were impoverished, did not speak English or had no one to care for them. Many of these patients had been abandoned by their families, an all-too-common practice at the time.

From 1891 to 1928, 1,131 Chinese laborers were also buried in block 14 of the cemetery, the historically Chinese section. As described by the Metro Council, thousands of people traveled by ship from southern China to the United States in the mid- to late 1800s. Many of these individuals performed the most arduous tasks of building the Pacific Northwest's infrastructure and economy while being underpaid for their work. The remains of approximately 800 Chinese men were unearthed from the cemetery in 1928 and 1941 and sent to China for reburial. In 1952, Multnomah County built the Morrison Building on block 14, then in 2002, it planned to demolish the building and sell the property. Several nonprofit groups, including the Oregon Chinese Consolidated Benevolent Association, informed the county in 2004 of their belief that block 14 still contained human remains. This was found to be true; 330 bodies had not been relocated to China. The building was removed, and block 14 was reconnected to the cemetery. A memorial garden is planned to honor those who were buried in block 14.

Also buried at the Lone Fir Cemetery is Charity Lamb, the first woman convicted of murder in the Oregon Territory. She was the eighth person incarcerated in Oregon and was nicknamed "Oregon's Lizzie Borden." She murdered her husband of seventeen years, Nathaniel, on May 13, 1854, striking him twice in the head with an axe while they sat at the dinner table with their six children. Nathaniel survived for two weeks after the attack.

Charity told the constable that she "did not mean to kill the critter, only intended to stun him." The local newspapers branded Charity "a monster" and described Nathaniel as "an industrious and quiet citizen, and had a good claim, which he improved considerably with his own hands." Charity was charged with premeditated, first-degree murder. At her trial, the Oregonian described Charity as "pale and sallow, and emaciated as a skeleton." Stories were told of extramarital affairs and domestic violence. Their children testified that Nathaniel frequently beat Charity, hit her with a hammer and tried to poison her. Charity's lawyers argued that the murder was done in self-defense and that she was a "monomaniac," obsessed with killing Nathaniel because of his frequent abuse. Charity was found guilty of second-degree murder, and the jury, sympathizing with Charity, urged leniency. At her sentencing, Charity said to the judge: "Well, I don't know that I murdered him. He was alive when I saw him last....Well, I struck him once; and then I threw the tool and run, to get out of the way. I knew he was going to kill me." The judge imposed the most lenient sentence possible: life in prison at the Oregon State Penitentiary. Ten years later, Charity was transferred to the Hawthorne Asylum, where facility inspectors documented her in 1865: "She sat knitting as the visiting party went through the hall, face imperturbably fixed in half smiling contentment, apparently as satisfied with her lot as the happiest of sane people with theirs." Charity died at the Asylum in 1879 at the age of sixty-one.

Legend has it that the ghosts of Merlotin, Lamb, the Asylum's dead and the 330 Chinese individuals left in Lone Fir Cemetery haunt the grounds. Their spirits have been reported wandering aimlessly around the cemetery.

The cemetery now hosts a Halloween event called "Graveyard Goodies," in which actors portray some of Lone Fir's better-known spirits and hand out candy.

2

VANCOUVER, WASHINGTON

PHANTOM SOLDIERS

Vancouver, Washington, is the largest suburb of Portland, Oregon, and lies just on the northern side of the Columbia River in Washington State. It is named for Captain George Vancouver of the British Royal Navy, who explored the Pacific Northwest from 1791 to 1795. From 1824 to the 1850s, Fort Vancouver, now a national historic site, served as the regional headquarters for the British Hudson's Bay Company's fur trading business. In 1849, after the United States took control of the area, the fort's military barracks were built, first called Camp Columbia, then Fort Vancouver Military Reservation and, finally, the Vancouver Barracks. The fort was used by the U.S. Army in protecting settlers traveling from the East Coast on the Oregon Trail. The fort was deactivated after World War II, but it is said that spirits there remain very active.

The fort's "officer's row" consisted of twenty-one white Victorian mansions, which housed the fort's officers and families. One of the mansions was named for Civil War hero and president Ulysses S. Grant, who served as quartermaster at the fort in the 1850s. Grant House is said to be haunted by Lieutenant Colonel Alfred Sully, who commanded the fort from 1874 until his death in 1879. It is said his footsteps can be heard pacing in the upper floor of the house. In one reported case of paranormal activity, Sully's ghost is said to have locked a telephone repair person in the house. In another instance, Sully's spirit is said to have told a visitor to the Grant House "I lived here before, and I am just looking around."

Photograph of an old door closure. *Courtesy of Pixabay.*

Two doors down from the Grant House is the Nelson House, where a blood-like substance has been seen dripping down the walls, and the grass is said to turn from green to brown four days each week.

Barrack no. 614 was used as a hospital and psychiatric ward beginning in 1884. Toilet seats are reported to open and close on their own, the front door locks and unlocks itself and disembodied voices and coughs can be heard. In the basement, which was used as the morgue and "blood-draining" area, an angry spirit is said to have chased people out of the building. On the third floor, where psychiatric patients were housed, screaming and laughing can be heard, and papers have reportedly floated and become stuck on the ceiling.

In 1982, pipes were being repaired in the auditorium's basement when several human skeletons were discovered. Although one was wearing trading beads, it was thought to be unlikely that the skeletons were those of Natives, as they generally buried their dead in canoes on islands in the nearby rivers or the opposite shore, not in the ground. While those Native remains would eventually decay and disappear, the cedar canoes would remain as monuments. The bodies found in the auditorium basement were simply found covered with dirt.

For ten years after the skeletons in the basement were discovered, soldiers heard strange, disembodied footsteps above and below the auditorium. In 1993, renovations began on the basement, and the new base commander was told of the bones. Contrary to earlier assessments, further investigations revealed the bones were, in fact, those of Natives who had worked and died there, dating back to when the British controlled the fort in the 1840s and 1850s. While White men's graves had been properly moved from the fort's burial ground and marked, Native bodies were left where they had been placed with no markers. In the late 1990s, the base held a traditional Native ceremony, giving proper burials to the dead. Following the ceremony, footsteps were no longer heard in the auditorium, though ghosts reportedly continued to reside in the barracks' headquarters.

In another haunting, the spirit of a nanny who cared for an officer's children, who was said to have been sexually assaulted by the officer and impregnated as a result, is said to be present. The officer denied any responsibility for the assault. "Nan," as the spirit is called, hanged herself from the building's bannister. The building is now home to a real estate company. Employees have reported hearing the disembodied shuffling of papers and other materials, and a desktop bell has been routinely rung even when no customers are present. The employees believe it is Nan's spirit.

3

TILLAMOOK, OREGON

"TERRIBLE TILLY"

The city of Tillamook, named for the local Native tribe, was incorporated in 1891 and lies in the heart of the Oregon Coast's dairy country. Though Tillamook is home to the century-old Tillamook Cheese Factory, ocean-front dairy farming is only one part of this area's history.

In 1788, Captain Robert Gray, while sailing on the ship *Lady Washington*, anchored in Tillamook Bay. The first settler, Joseph Champion, made his home here in 1851. In the early years, the town was known as Lincoln. In 1878, the U.S. government decided a lighthouse was needed to guide ships around Tillamook Head, Oregon, as perilous weather and geography made seafaring dangerous. Congress allocated $50,000 (equivalent to $1.3 million in 2020) for its construction. The head is a 1,200-foot-high, 15-million-year-old, steep, rocky bluff jutting into the ocean. The Tillamook Rock Lighthouse was to be built on the head, but as the head was frequently shrouded in fog, the lighthouse was, instead, built on a large piece of basalt rock located a mile offshore, known as "the Rock." Despite its innocuous appearance, the lighthouse quickly became known as Terrible Tilly for the strong storms, arduous working conditions, ghostly legends, mysteries and myths surrounding it.

Members of the Native Tillamook tribe warned the lighthouse builders that the basalt rock location was cursed by their gods and haunted by evil spirits; the Tillamook avoided it. Tragedy struck almost immediately. On September 18, 1879, Master Mason John R. Trewavas, the first surveyor of the location, lost his footing and was swept out to sea; his remains were

Photograph of Tillamook, Oregon Coast, 1941. *Courtesy of the Miriam and Ira D. Wallach Photography Collection, New York Public Library.*

never found. Knowing the difficulties of the location, locals refused to work on the lighthouse's construction. A new surveyor, Charles A. Ballantyne, was appointed and had to hire a construction crew from outside the area. The crew was housed at Cape Disappointment to ensure locals would not scare them away.

Constructing the lighthouse was no easy feat. On January 2, 1880, a terrible storm struck the Rock. Provisions and tools were swept away by enormous waves, and the nine lighthouse construction workers hunkered down as best they could. Sixteen days after the storm hit, despite rumors of their demise, the workers were found in good health but in great need of food and supplies.

On January 3, 1881, with the lighthouse close to completion but not yet lit, the British, 1,200-ton ship *Lupatia* wrecked on the Rock. It had been caught in strong winds and heavy fog, causing poor visibility. The lighthouse construction crew heard shouts of "hard aport," masts and rigging creaking and saw faint lights as the ship struggled to avoid the Rock. The *Lupatia* sank, killing all sixteen crew members on board. Twelve bodies washed ashore, while the other four were never found. The only survivor was the crew's Australian shepherd puppy.

After 575 days of construction, and at a cost of $123,493 (equivalent to $3.1 million in 2020), the lighthouse went into operation on January 21, 1881. Four lightkeepers at a time were assigned to work the light; they were responsible for maintaining the light, which guided ships through the treacherous waters.

Since beginning operations, tales of paranormal occurrences have surrounded Terrible Tilly. James A. Gibbs, who served at the lighthouse from 1945 to 1946, said he had been warned by the three other lightkeepers that ghosts inhabited the lighthouse. Gibbs reported hearing disembodied footsteps, the feeling of air brushing by his throat and the sounds of moaning. Gibbs also said that he and the other lightkeepers once saw an eerie, lifeless ghost ship drifting aimlessly near the rocks, only to turn around and head back to sea. The lightkeepers reported the incident to the U.S. Coast Guard, but no ship could be identified.

Unattributed ghost stories from the early twentieth century include the spirit of a former lighthouse keeper, which is said to be a malevolent poltergeist that chases and attacks people. A benevolent spirit is also said to haunt the lighthouse; the ghost of a lightkeeper who wanted to be—and was—buried on the lighthouse grounds.

On September 1, 1957, the lighthouse was deactivated, made obsolete by new technology. Strangely fitting, from 1980 to 1999, Terrible Tilly was used as a columbarium, storing urns with cremated human remains. It is now part of the lovely Ecola State Park.

4

MANZANITA, OREGON

PIRATES, GHOSTS AND BURIED TREASURE

Named for the fruit that grows in the area, Manzanita is a quiet, beautiful costal town whose name means "little apple" in Spanish. In addition to the name's pleasant meaning, another description for the area should probably be "haunted."

Neahkahnie Mountain, just north of the town of Manzanita, Oregon, juts 1,600 feet above the coastline. Natives thought the mountain was an inspiring viewpoint, where their most powerful god lived; they named it *Ne*, "place of," and *Ekahni*, meaning "supreme deity." The first European to land there was Sir Frances Drake, who docked his ship in 1579, during his sail around the globe.

The mountain, which is often shrouded in fog, is the source of many supernatural tales and is said to be haunted by a number of ghosts. The 2005 horror movie *The Fog*, which tells of fog bringing vindictive, ghostly mariners who were murdered 134 years prior, was set on a fictional island off the North Oregon Coast. The story loosely resembles the real Neahkahnie murders, which occurred some 312 years earlier and spawned many ghostly tales.

Chinook Natives have a strong belief in powerful spirits and a particular interest in death, specifically the fate of the soul in the world of ghosts. Many Natives also believe that spirits coming back after death spell doom for the living and are to be avoided. There is a belief that when a person dies, a "malignant influence" is released and able to return to earth as a ghost. These spirits haunt burial grounds and may plague the living.

As legend has it, Spanish treasure is buried on or near Neahkahnie Mountain and is guarded by ghosts. In 1693, a Spanish vessel wrecked on the Nehalem Spit at the base of the mountain. Thirty survivors made it to the beach, carrying a treasure chest in a longboat. The men dragged the chest onto the mountain and dug a hole. The captain, knowing that Natives feared disturbing graves and ghosts, shot his Black Caribbean enslaved man and buried him on top of the treasure. The captain also shot and chased away other crew members, possibly burying them with the treasure. The captain and remaining crew rowed toward Mexico. The Natives never dug up the treasure.

Careful archaeological analysis concluded that the Spanish ship *Santo Cristo de Burgos*, which sailed from Manila in 1693 (headed to California), likely wrecked on the Nehalem Spit in 1693. Portland State University researchers cited local Native tales describing European sailors coming ashore and burying a large chest on Neahkahnie Mountain. Further, the researchers noted strange blocks of dried beeswax with dots, lines, markings, indecipherable words and the letters "DE"—meaning "of" in Spanish and part of the Burgos's name—have been found on the southwestern face of the mountain. Some treasure hunters have surmised that these are indicators of where the treasure is buried, as the Spanish shipped beeswax around the Pacific Ocean in the late 1600s for use in Catholic masses. A tsunami, resulting from the 1700 Cascadia Subduction Zone earthquake, may have struck the wreck of the *Santo Cristo de Burgos*, scattering the beeswax around the area.

The researchers also discussed the earliest known Euro-American treasure seeker, John Hobson, who came to the Clatsop Plains in 1843. Hobson reportedly learned from the local Natives of an abundance of beeswax blocks that had been washed ashore on nearby beaches from an old shipwreck. He also heard of gold and silver coins that were buried nearby, suggesting the buried treasure may have come from the same wreck as the beeswax. The Natives told Hobson tales of sailors carrying a chest onto Neahkahnie Mountain, placing sacks of money in it and burying the chest with the corpse of an enslaved man the sailors had killed. Finding no evidence, in 1848, Hobson concluded the lore was untrue.

At least three treasure hunters have lost their lives on Neahkahnie Mountain. In 1931, Charles Wood and his son Lynn dug a thirty-foot-deep hole into the mountain without adding supports; a cave-in killed them both. In 1990, two treasure hunters rappelled down Neahkahnie Mountain to search for the treasure from the water in an inflatable raft. Waves swept them

Photograph of an old tapestry. *Author's collection.*

into a cave, and both men were stranded. One of them, Samuel Logan, was pulled back out to sea by another wave and drowned. It is not clear what became of the other treasure hunter. Dreams of treasure prompted generations of treasure seekers to riddle Neahkahnie Mountain's landscape with pits and trenches, giving it the nickname "mountain of a thousand holes." From 1967 to 1999, the state of Oregon formally gave treasure hunters permits to search for treasure on state-owned lands. However, Oregon's "Treasure Trove" statute was repealed in 1999, making treasure hunting illegal on Neahkahnie Mountain and nearby beaches.

Legend has it that the treasure, still where the Spanish sailors buried it, is guarded by the ghosts of the enslaved man, other possible murder victims, their murderers and the treasure hunters who died attempting to locate the treasure. Some of these spirits may be seeking vengeance for the violent, tragic deaths they suffered, the sudden and unexpected accidents they experienced or the improper burials they received. Or perhaps they feel attached to and protective of the treasure. As the Natives said, these ghosts are omens of death and are to be avoided. As such, the strange beeswax blocks may be signals from the spirits to stay away.

5

CANNON BEACH, OREGON

"BANDAGE MAN"

The Lewis and Clark Expedition traveled to Cannon Beach in 1806. The town that would become Cannon Beach was first named Elk Creek for the nearby Elk Creek River. In 1846, a cannon from the shipwrecked USS *Shark* washed ashore, and the area was soon referred to as Cannon Beach. This became the area's official name in 1922. Cannon Beach is described by many as a lovely, peaceful setting by the sea—that is, except for the ghostly Bandage Man who is said to haunt the area.

The story of Bandage Man, as reflected in media and legends, begins with a secluded stretch of Highway 101 in Cannon Beach, where the Bandage Man makes his presence known to unfortunate residents and visitors. He is said to haunt the Highway 26 Overpass at the junction of Highways 26 and 101. The legend dates back to the late 1950s or early 1960s, beginning with the story of a young couple who sat parked in their pickup truck near the beach. Suddenly, the couple felt the truck move as if someone had climbed into the cargo bed. They turned, looked through the back window and saw a disfigured man covered in bloody bandages rocking back and forth. They reported that he started beating on the back window and roof. They raced away, down the highway, and the bandaged man disappeared.

Others have since reported seeing Bandage Man jumping into open truck beds and convertible cars' backseats. Still others say they've seen him walking along the beach, down Highway 101 and on a short road called "Bandage Man Road." There are also stories of Bandage Man smashing the windows of a local business and even eating someone's dog. These people believe

Photograph of Cannon Beach, Oregon Coast, 2015. *Courtesy of Danielamorescalchi0, Pixabay.*

he's the tormented ghost of a logger who died in a horrific accident while working in the area. They report that the smells of rotting flesh and bloody bandages linger even after Bandage Man vanishes.

Another legend reports that Bandage Man was a logger in the 1930s who was badly injured on the job. He was wrapped in bandages and sent away in an ambulance. However, that ambulance fell victim to a landslide while en route to the hospital on old Highway 101. When the rescue crew arrived at the landslide location, the injured logger was reportedly gone. Evidence indicates a portion of Highway 101 was formerly curvy but later straightened as part of repairs due to a landslide. Other witness accounts say the Bandage Man is wrapped in dirty bandages, his body broken and misshapen, with his arms and legs extruding from his body at odd angles. He tries to jump into passing cars, which is why locals avoid driving down the Highway 26 Overpass after dark.

Bandage Man has been the subject of a 1974 University of Oregon "Northwest Folklore" research study titled "The Bandage Man Legend: A Cannon Beach Legend." The study explores the haunted tales and legends that have been passed down since the 1950s. He was the focus of a 2003 horror-comedy film titled *Bandage Man*, directed by multiple-award-winning

Photograph of Cannon Beach, Oregon Coast, 2019. *Courtesy of RevMac, Pixabay.*

Irish filmmaker Ivan Kavanagh. The movie stays relatively true to the legend. It tells of a man who regularly travels on the Highway 26 Overpass at night, despite warnings not to do so. As it turns out, the man is looking for Bandage Man, who he visits weekly to provide him with another dog to eat.

The most recent documented sighting of Bandage Man occurred in early 2019. The female witness described being awakened by the feeling that someone was watching her. She opened her eyes to see a man standing by her bed who appeared to be covered in toilet paper. Half asleep, she described the wrapping as loosely hanging from his face, going all the way down his body. The moonlight illuminated Bandage Man from the knees up. The witness was scared and kept thinking, "This isn't real, this isn't real, I'm dreaming." But she wasn't. She says he then gestured toward her, lunging with his upper body. She squeezed her eyes shut, and when she opened them again, Bandage Man was gone. She said this event was the only—and scariest—"night terror" she had ever experienced.

It could be that the Bandage Man's ghost is haunting Cannon Beach due to the unexpected, tragic accident that is thought to have taken his life. Perhaps his suffering ties him to this world. He may feel he has unfinished business, or he may be searching for living loved ones.

Those who venture to the secluded Highway 26 Overpass in Cannon Beach should exercise caution, as Bandage Man may pay them a visit.

6

SEASIDE, OREGON

SALTY SÉANCE

In 1806, a group from the Lewis and Clark Expedition built a salt-making cairn, or oven, at the site that would become Seaside, Oregon. Natives have long inhabited Seaside, and the area grew slowly, with the city incorporated in 1899. It is a major tourism center, with fun carnival rides and beautiful hotels. However, there may be something not-so-fun lurking in the town's aquarium.

The Seaside Aquarium, described by many as charming and fun, is the oldest privately owned aquarium on the West Coast. It was built in 1924 as a saltwater bathhouse and became an aquarium in 1937. Legend says it is haunted.

In the 1920s, the town of Seaside had three "natatoriums," or large indoor pools. One of the three was the Seaside Baths Natatorium, which would later become the Seaside Aquarium. A common phrase of the time was, "I'll see you at the Nat!" The facility contained a large indoor swimming pool that was filled with saltwater pumped directly from the Pacific Ocean through a pipe that is still visible today. The water was heated, creating a warm saltwater swimming experience. There was a big fountain in the middle of the pool that people sat on, and there was a children's wading pool with a large window facing the ocean. Bands would play at the natatorium, and people would gather for fun. In 1932, the Great Depression forced the Seaside Baths Natatorium to close.

Following its closing, the facility was first used as a salmon farm, then as a location to watch wrestling matches. Both efforts failed. Since 1937,

Photograph of Seaside, Oregon, 1941. *Courtesy of the Miriam and Ira D. Wallach Photography Collection, New York Public Library.*

many witnesses have said the former natatorium is haunted by unknown spirits—perhaps those of rumored drowning victims who were said to have died while swimming at the natatorium. Their spirits may remain to haunt the location of their deaths.

The building was remodeled and opened as the Seaside Aquarium in 1937, using the same pipe that was installed in the 1920s to fill the aquarium tanks. Admission prices were fifteen cents for adults and ten cents for children. In 1938, the Sea Water Apartments were added to the third floor, where they remained in use until 1970, when a period of renovation lasting thirty-five years began. It is on this third floor where paranormal activities are said to exist. While the public can't access this area, it has been described as "creepy." There are rickety and tilting floors, as well as ghostly remnants of former residents' lives, including old beds and furniture, fixtures and a board displaying the names of the last residents. An overwhelming sense of foreboding is said to envelop the third floor, and employees have reported hearing disembodied voices at night. Others have reported hearing footsteps, knocking and other unexplained noises.

Another interesting connection between the aquarium and strange occurrences involves the 2011 Tohoku earthquake and tsunami in Japan. A boat that was swept away during this event floated across the Pacific Ocean and washed ashore in Washington State, carrying trapped, live fish. The fish were put on display at the Seaside Aquarium. The magnitude 9.1 earthquake was the most powerful to ever strike Japan, killing 15,899 people, with 2,529 people missing. Could this strange series of events have something to do with the reported paranormal activities at the aquarium, or is this simply an odd coincidence? You decide.

7

WARRENTON, OREGON

SPECTRAL FORT STEVENS

The Clatsop tribe of Natives inhabited the Warrenton area for centuries; the county in which Warrenton sits was named for them. Warrenton, a fishing, logging and modern retail center, was founded in the 1870s by D.K. Warren, and it was incorporated in 1899. It was built on tidal flats, protected from the Columbia River by walls that were built by Chinese laborers. Although the walls protected the area from overflowing water, there may be nothing protecting the unprepared from the spirits that are said to inhabit the nearby fort.

Fort Stevens was built in 1863, during the Civil War, and was in service until 1947. It was named for General Isaac Stevens, a former governor of the Washington Territory. It was one of three major historic forts built to guard the mouth of the Columbia River; it was intended to protect against a possible British invasion from Canada if England decided to join the Civil War on the Confederate side. It was originally an "earthwork" fort, mainly made from dirt and surrounded by a moat and drawbridge. In 1897, a massive refortification program took place, resulting in the addition of eight concrete batteries, including mortars and long- and short-range rifles. The fort was on alert during several wars, including the Native Wars, Civil War, Spanish-American War, World War I and World War II.

During World War II, there were approximately 2,500 men stationed at Fort Stevens. In April 1942, four months after the Japanese attack on Pearl Harbor, the American "Doolittle Raid," named for its leader Lieutenant Colonel James H. Doolittle, managed to attack the Japanese mainland with

Photograph of
Warrenton, Oregon
Fort Stevens.
*Courtesy of the Library
of Congress.*

sixteen B-25 bombers. The Japanese were shocked and planned an attack on the continental United States on June 21, 1942. The Japanese long-range submarine *I-25* maneuvered through a fishing fleet and avoided minefields on the Columbia River. The submarine's crew fired seventeen shells from its five-and-a-half-inch deck gun at what Japanese commander Meiji Tagami thought was a submarine base. Instead, it was Fort Stevens, which remains the only mainland U.S. Military installation shelled by a foreign enemy warship since the War of 1812. Soldiers at the fort later remembered the attack causing confusion, resulting in a "real mad house." The fort didn't return fire, as the submarine was inaccurately identified as being out of range, and the commander "didn't want to give away the precise location of the defenses." One U.S. soldier cut his head while rushing to his battle station. The ten-inch guns of the fort's Battery Russell were damaged by shells, as was the fort's baseball diamond and a power line. The *I-25*'s shells left craters on the beach and marshland around the fort. The attack ended at midnight, and the submarine sailed away.

Many of the fort's bunkers and batteries still exist. Touring these abandoned, historic structures has been described by some as "unnerving." Visitors and staff have reported seeing the ghosts of soldiers, one in full battle gear, one carrying a long knife and one carrying a flashlight, wandering the grounds, appearing to be in search of possible enemy soldiers. Two appear to be dressed in Civil War–era uniforms, while the other is dressed in World War II–era clothing. A man described walking around the grounds and seeing a soldier dressed in a World War II uniform. They nodded to each other, and when the man turned around to again see the out-of-place soldier, he was gone. Disembodied voices and footsteps can be heard, and glowing spirit orbs have been seen in the old guardhouse. The stories of these ghosts' presence are usually connected with unexplainable noises and rushes of cold air.

The most haunted spot is said to be Battery Russel, where cold spots, strange noises and ghosts are reported. Could it be that the dramatic event of the submarine attack caused spirits to continue to defend the battery and fort? The Travel Channel program *Ghost Adventures* visited the fort in 2019 to investigate stories of the fort's haunting. One witness, while touring the fort with a friend, described encountering spirits at the battery. He said he had never experienced a supernatural event before. While touring, he sensed "echoes of pain and fear" and believed he was being stared at. He didn't tell his friend but could tell he sensed something out of the ordinary as well. As he approached one of the enclosed bunkers, he stopped, not able to move any further. He wanted to know what was inside, but his friend pleaded with him not to enter. An image flashed through his mind of someone standing inside, holding a knife, waiting for someone to enter. As he experienced this, he was knocked backward, to the ground. It seemed that he was being warned to leave. His friend, only a few feet away, anxiously said, "We need to go!" They broke into a run down the hill to get to their van. He turned to see his friend shaking and crying. Before he could ask if his friend was OK, the friend asked, "did you see the guy in fatigues in the bunker holding a knife?" They both had seen the same thing. His friend also said he had seen another soldier hiding in the bushes as they ran.

Other witnesses have described hearing faint wailing, as if someone is in pain; the hushed yelling of someone giving orders; a disembodied voice saying, "get out"; and feeling as if someone was watching them. Others described hearing disembodied footsteps moving across the gravel outside their tent in what is the current camping area.

When you visit Fort Stevens, take care, as you never know who you might run into.

8

Astoria, Oregon

"Ghostoria"

Hauntings on Land

The beautiful, rustic, waterfront city of Astoria has been the center of reported paranormal activity for well over a century. The 2007 horror movie *Cthulhu*, based on H.P. Lovecraft's 1936 book *Shadow Over Innsmouth*, was filmed in Astoria and based on Astoria legends. Most recently, in 2019, the Travel Channel program *Ghost Adventures* produced a multi-episode segment focusing on Astoria and the Graveyard of the Pacific. Instead of Astoria, a better name for the city may be Ghostoria, as many ghosts seem to inhabit the area.

Astoria lays at the mouth of the Columbia River and has a rich and colorful (blood-red, some would say) history. Although other towns may make this claim to fame, Astoria was once said to be the "most wicked place on earth." Gambling houses, brothels, saloons and worse were common in the town in the late 1800s. Unsuspecting sailors were shanghaied from local bars, boardinghouses and even while walking down the sidewalk, taken through underground tunnels to serve on ships in need of crews. Women were kidnapped to work as prostitutes. Thousands of shipwrecks, claiming countless lives, occurred in the nearby hazardous waters of this dangerous, fog-enshrouded part of the Pacific Coast. Bodies of unidentified drowning victims washed ashore nearby. It is said that Astoria's longstanding brutal history makes it prime haunting territory for lingering spirits.

Photograph of the Astoria-Megler Bridge, Oregon, 2011. *Courtesy of Malasoca, Pixabay.*

UPPERTOWN FIREHOUSE MUSEUM

Astoria burned down in 1883 and again in 1922. The Astoria Fire House No. 2, now known as the Uppertown Firehouse Museum, was originally built in 1895 as the North Pacific Brewing Company. It operated as a brewery until Prohibition, when it was then used to make an unsuccessful nonalcoholic beer called "Maltona." Next, the building housed the Far West Milk Company, making condensed milk, until it, too, went out of business. In 1928, it was converted into the town fire station and served in that role until 1960. It is now a fascinating, historic museum, housing firefighting equipment from the period between 1879 and 1963, including hand-pulled, horse-drawn and motorized fire engines; firefighting arm badges from across America; and other memorabilia and photographs. The museum was listed in the National Register of Historic Places in 1984.

Witnesses have reported hearing strange sounds and disembodied footsteps on the third floor. The ghost of a fireman who reportedly fell to his death while sliding down a fire pole in the 1920s has been seen. Likewise, the spirit of a sleepwalking fireman who reportedly also fell to his death in the 1920s was reported by former occupants of the building as standing over them while they tried to sleep. Other firefighting apparitions, thought to be keeping an eye out for a third town fire, have been reported, as have lockers rattling by themselves, eerie noises and disembodied footsteps coming from the third floor.

FLAVEL HOUSES

One of Astoria's most famous rumored haunts is the lovely Victorian Flavel House Museum. Prominent local pilot boat captain and businessman Captain George Flavel had the house built in 1884. The grand house comprises almost twelve thousand square feet, with six fireplaces, fourteen-foot-high ceilings on the first floor and twelve-foot-high ceilings on the second.

Captain George and Mary Flavel had three children: Nellie, Katie and George C. (also a captain). Nellie and Katie lived in the house with their parents, but George C. never did. The Flavel family had an important impact on the city of Astoria from the late nineteenth century until 2018. The last descendent of Captain George and Mary Flavel, their great-granddaughter Mary Louise Flavel, died in November 2018, closing a long and complex history of Astoria's famous maritime family.

On the first floor of the house, it is said one can hear disembodied voices and phantom music, thought to be that of daughters Katie and Nellie, the latter of whom was a classically trained pianist and performed with the Organists' Guild of Portland. The library room is said to be haunted by an unhappy presence, while the second floor is inhabited by the apparition of a woman that disappears once it is seen. One of the Flavel's bedrooms is reported to have an ever-present floral scent, although no flowers are there. Captain Flavel's spirit has been seen in his bedroom, only to vanish once it is noticed. When a witness visited the Flavel House and asked about ghosts in the museum, a staff member reportedly responded that when she ventured up the spire (a lookout one can only access by a narrow staircase in the attic), she was pushed toward the descending staircase by an unseen presence. The staff member refused to go back to the lookout.

Astoria has a second grand Flavel house, which was built in 1901 and owned by Captain George's son, George C., and his wife, Winona, and later inherited by their son Harry M. Harry M., who lived in this house with his

Photograph of an antique room. *Courtesy of Pixabay*.

wife, Florence, and their two children, Harry S. and Mary Louise. In 1947, when Harry S. was twenty, it is said neighbor Fred Fulton heard screams for help coming from the house. Fearing the worst, the neighbor stormed into the house and found Harry's mother Florence locked in an upstairs room, screaming to be let out. Harry S. attacked the neighbor with a hatchet, hitting the banister and cutting the neighbor's arm. Florence declined to press charges, and both she and Mary Louise testified that neighbor Fulton was drunk and broke into their house. They claimed Harry S. acted in self-defense, and he was let go. He earned the nickname "Hatchet Harry" after this incident.

Thirty-six years later, in 1983, it was reported that Harry S. was walking two dogs when a car sped past. Harry S., irritated at its speed, hit it with the metal dog leash. The driver stopped and approached Harry, who stabbed him with a knife. Once again charged with assault, Harry lost his case. He; his sister, Mary Louise; and his mother, Florence, packed up and disappeared, leaving the house to rot. In October 1990, Harry was arrested in Pennsylvania for stealing a hotel's towels. His family fled again, only to be arrested in 1991 in Massachusetts and extradited back to Oregon. He spent a year in jail before being released and disappearing again; he died in 2010. Harry's mother, Florence, died just before he did. It's said that Harry's sister, Mary Louise, refused to pay for his burial, and Harry's body remained at a morgue for nine months. Shortly after his death, a black funeral banner was mysteriously draped over the balcony of the family's abandoned house, left by an unknown mourner.

Photograph of the Flavel House, 2014. *Courtesy of DyeAnnaBee, Pixabay.*

The county later took ownership of the house, cleaned and repaired it. It found three-foot-deep piles of one-hundred-year-old newspapers, magazines, unopened mail and stacks of items spread in disarray throughout the house. A twelve-inch-long knife was found in the basement stairwell, and empty plastic jugs of bleach hung by their necks from ceiling to floor. A 1950s woman's bathing suit was found in a pink bathroom, while a dead dog was found in the refrigerator. The house was bought by a private owner in 2015, who restored it to its former glory and says it isn't haunted. But others refer to it as the most haunted house in Oregon and say it's haunted by the ghosts of Mary Louise, Florence and Harry S.

LIBERTY THEATER

The historic Liberty Theater, located in the heart of Astoria and housed on the site of the former Weinhard-Astoria Hotel, in the Astor building, was the first theater that was re-established after the destructive Astoria fire of 1922. At its opening in 1925, it was viewed as symbolic of the city's rebirth. Its architecture is Italian Renaissance, with an auditorium featuring twelve mural-style oil paintings by local artist Joseph Knowles, depicting Venetian canal scenes. In 1984, the building was added to the National Register of Historic Places, and from 2000 to 2006, the theater underwent a complete restoration. It is now a venue for performing arts and live entertainment. In the 1920s, the theater hosted such luminaries as Duke Ellington, Jack Benny, Guy Lombardo and the infamous Al Capone. The Travel Channel's *Ghost Adventures* visited the Liberty Theater in 2019 as part of its four-part series focusing on the Graveyard of the Pacific.

The ghost of "Handsome Paul" is said to haunt the theater, reportedly dressed in a "white tuxedo and a panama hat." He has been known to open, close and slam doors and make other noises. Other ghostly tales include two men wearing top hats that are seen near the elevator, the spirit of an elderly woman, soda fountains and popcorn machines turning on in the middle of the night, objects moving of their own accord, doorknobs rattling, knobs on appliances unscrewing themselves, the sound of knocking on doors and mysterious voices.

The Liberty Theater sits on top of underground tunnels, which encompass almost two city blocks. Some of these tunnels were used to shanghai and kidnap unsuspecting sailors and women and are said to

Photograph of old theater seats, 2015. *Courtesy of Cotsfan, Pixabay.*

be haunted. Some theater employees say they are afraid to go into the basement because of what may be waiting there in the dark.

HAUNTINGS UNDERGROUND: TUNNELS

The Astoria underground tunnel system serves as a major backdrop for reported paranormal activity within the city. After the 1922 fire destroyed downtown Astoria, the city was rebuilt fifteen feet higher, moving it farther from the Columbia River and Pacific Ocean. This created underground alleys, streets and rooms and expanded the already existing tunnels.

Between 1850 and the 1940s, countless men were reportedly shanghaied to serve unwillingly aboard ships. Many of these kidnappings were perpetrated by Bunko Kelly, the infamous shanghaier who kidnapped men and women in Portland throughout the late nineteenth century. Kelly called Astoria "the wickedest city in the world, worse than New Orleans." These events were featured in an early-1930s series of articles by *Oregonian* newspaper reporter Steward Holbrook and in other sources. Herman Melville, the author of the 1851 classic *Moby Dick*, described shanghaiers as "sharks, rats, and other vermin, who took the form of landlords, barkeepers, and prostitutes to prey on helpless sailors."

Shanghaiing was widely practiced in Astoria during the late nineteenth century. On the north side of Astoria's Commercial Street, between Fourteenth and Fifteenth Streets, was Bridget Grant's seaman's boardinghouse. It was in business for thirty years, and Astorians knew it to be active in shanghaiing. Jim Turk, who is credited with bringing the

Photograph of Astoria, Oregon wall mural. *Author's collection.*

practice of shanghaiing to Oregon, ran a seaman's boardinghouse on the south side of Commercial Street, between Fifteenth and Sixteenth Streets. There, he and his sons engaged in shanghaiing in the late 1800s.

There are many stories of Astoria shanghaiings that were relayed by victims and witnesses. In 1877, twenty-year-old Richard Lewis described having a great time at the Astor Saloon and having too much to drink. While getting ready to head to his boardinghouse, Richard recalled hearing men's voices. Next thing he knew, he was lying in a dark, wet tunnel under the town's buildings and sidewalks. Richard was unwillingly taken aboard a ship, where he was put to work as a crew member.

In her book *The Trail Led North: Mont Hawthorne's Story*, noted historian Martha McKeown, a native Astorian and descendant of covered-wagon pioneers, recounted the story of her uncle Mont Hawthorne, a newcomer to Astoria in the 1880s. McKeown described how Hawthorne was warned by a neighbor of prior shanghaiing in Astoria and, henceforth, always carried a gun with him. One night, unknown assailants attempted to break into his cabin in what he believed to be an attempted shanghaiing. They hastily departed when he shot through the door seven times. Even Astoria's nineteenth-century Methodist minister George Grannis was almost shanghaied. After ringing his church's bells on a Sunday, Grannis had an overcoat thrown over his head by one shanghaier and his arms pinned to his side by another. He fought back, kicking one of his assailants and headbutting the other, causing the three to tumble down the stairs. The assailants fled the scene.

There are many reports describing disembodied voices, footsteps, strange smells and other unexplained phenomena occurring within the tunnels. Witnesses suggest that the spirits of shanghaied victims may linger within underground Astoria, bound to Earth by their sudden, unexpected and often violent deaths.

Hauntings at Sea

Nautical disasters have added to the ghostly legends that surround the Astoria area. The sheer number of shipwrecks (more than two thousand) and countless lives lost in the graveyard is overwhelming. Practically every type of eighteenth-, nineteenth- and early twentieth-century ship of American, British, Canadian, Chilean, Dutch, French and other ownership wrecked or suffered an accident in the graveyard. Even the USS *Arizona* battleship collided with a fishing boat on July 26, 1934 (seven years before it was sunk at Pearl Harbor), killing two fishermen.

The *General Warren*

One wreck involved the sidewheeler *General Warren*, which struck land in heavy weather at the Clatsop Spit on January 31, 1852, with forty-two men on board. The spit was a low sand beach, subject to extensive shifting, which was often invisible to the naked eye and covered by water. No lighthouse existed there, but the necessity for one had been urged repeatedly. When the *General Warren* began leaking after striking the spit, Captain Charles Thompson launched a small boat with ten men on board to seek help in Astoria.

Photograph of a paddlewheel boat, Astoria, Oregon. *Courtesy of Pixabay.*

On reaching Astoria, the crew sought and received help from Captain Beard of the steamer *George and Martha*. When the combined crew returned to the scene of the disaster, to their horror, they found no remnants of the wreck, passengers or crew. Thirty-two perished, the only survivors being the ten who sought help. Two victims' bodies washed ashore: a newlywed couple on their way to San Francisco for their honeymoon. It was reported that the groom had $160 in his jacket pocket, and the bride had a gold ring, engraved with a heart, on her left ring finger. They were holding hands when they were found washed ashore.

Given the history of the graveyard, it doesn't take much of an imagination to see the spirits of the newlyweds haunting the area in which they died. Could the winds, which seem to carry whispers, voices and moans, be carrying the words of the newlyweds' ghosts? It could be that their frantic efforts to stay alive, together with the shock of the tragedy and inevitability of death, would leave the victims' spirits restless. Two years later, in 1854, the *Warren*'s entire shattered frame washed ashore, sixty miles north of Clatsop.

THE J.C. COUSINS

The sixty-six-foot-long schooner *J.C. Cousins*, built in 1863, was formerly a luxury private yacht and, later, starting in 1881, operated as one of the two Astoria pilot boats. On October 6, 1883, the crew of four sailed off Clatsop Spit to await ships needing to be guided across the ever-dangerous bar. All appeared normal at first, but by late afternoon, things became strange. The *Cousins* was observed to be on the move, but it wasn't clear why, as there were no ships in need of assistance. Further, the *Cousins* was sailing through the treacherous breakers at the edge of the channel rather than the calm water a few dozen yards away. It cleared the breakers, heading to sea, but then a few miles offshore, it turned around and headed back to the bar again. When it got there, it once again turned around and headed back to the open ocean. It continued this erratic pattern until darkness fell. Some described it as seeming "possessed."

The next morning, a group of worried Astorians stood on the shore, watching the *Cousins* continuing its strange back and forth across the Columbia. The Astorians wondered aloud if this odd behavior was somehow linked to the treacherous "graveyard of ships." Around 1:00 p.m., the *Cousins* headed back toward land, this time, making no attempt to turn back around. Described as "churning through the surf with sails rigged and full of wind," the *Cousins* slammed onto the beach and tilted over onto its side. The onlookers ran to help but couldn't get near the wreck until several hours later at low tide. Nothing had moved on the deck of the *J.C. Cousins*; the ship looked lifeless.

When the Astorians reached the *Cousins*, it is said they were stunned to find it empty and deserted. Both lifeboats were gone, and all the paperwork was missing from the wheelhouse, suggesting the vessel had been deliberately abandoned. There was no sign of the crew, and none of them were ever heard from again, despite search efforts. Later, one of the *Cousins*'s two lifeboats washed ashore, but the oars were still lashed, indicating it had probably been washed overboard and not used to escape.

Locals started speculating as to the cause of this strange event. One theory was that one crew member, a Mr. Zeiber—little known to anyone in town—had been hired by the *J.C. Cousins*'s competitors as a "rat" to murder the crew members and wreck the ship. The *Cousins* was in competition with prominent Astorian Captain George Flavel's nautical monopoly. Some mariners, on returning to Astoria from ports in East Asia, claimed to have seen Zeiber there, alive and well. Other more fanciful theories, focused on the graveyard's habit of swallowing ships and claiming lives, were discussed at local taverns. These theories included a sea monster, giant squid, whale or shark getting the men or a mutiny in which the crew members murdered each other. Astoria is home to a significant number of proud Finnish Americans, and one of the "sea monsters" discussed may have been the "Tursas," a Finnish mythical being that is said to be a gargantuan, fierce octopus-type creature related to the mythical kraken. It was also suggested that it could have been a ghost ship bearing down on the *Cousins*, frightening the crew so badly that they crashed looking for a way off the boat.

There are more logical conclusions, such as the crew panicking and entering one of the lifeboats, only to have it go down with all on board. It could have been an accident, adverse weather conditions, waves, alcohol, exhaustion, suicide or piracy. It could have been "fata morgana," usually experienced on land (seeing water on land, a mirage, where there is none), leading the crew to see things that were not there. This phenomenon has been reported at sea before; mariners believe they see, for example, a beautiful tropical island, jump into the ocean to head for it and disappear. But if one of these logical theories is correct, why did the *Cousins* sail back and forth erratically for twelve to twenty-four hours? Perhaps it was instead "calenture," the irresistible impulse to jump into the sea, usually (though not always) brought on after a week or more of voyaging with no contact with land. Some sailors have reported imagining the sea to be a green field and wishing to jump onto it. The forward motion of the ship seems to enhance calenture. Others have reported "imaginary voices" encouraging them to jump in.

Whatever the cause, the mystery of the *J.C. Cousins* has not been solved in over 137 years. But according to the State of Washington's Department of Archeology and Historic Preservation, the *Cousins* was not the only ship to have its crew disappear. More than ten ships have gone down in the graveyard with no trace of their crew and, sometimes, no trace of the ship itself. The following are ten such vessels:

- November 20, 1852, schooner *Michigan*, unknown number of dead: Left Astoria for San Francisco with a cargo of lumber and a crew of nine. Shortly thereafter, a heavy gale hit the coast. Neither the *Michigan* nor its crew were heard from again.
- December 21, 1859, schooner *Rambler*, four dead: Washed up on Clatsop Spit, upside down. The *Rambler* left Neah Bay (in northernmost Washington State) for San Francisco with peltries (untreated pelts) and oil after fur trading with Natives to the north. No trace of the crew was ever found.
- December 27, 1860, bark *Leonese*, nine dead: Washed up on Clatsop Spit, upside down. No trace of the crew was ever found.
- November 22, 1875, schooner *Sunshine*, twenty-five dead: Washed up on Washington State's Long Beach Peninsula, just north of Astoria, upside down. No trace of the people on board was ever found.
- October 24, 1888, barkentine *Makah*, eleven dead: Washed up on Tillamook Head, capsized. The *Makah* had been en route from Port Discovery, Washington, just north of Seattle, to Sydney, Australia, with lumber. No sign of the crew was ever found.
- January 4, 1890, schooner *Dearborn*, unknown number of dead: Discovered capsized but afloat off the mouth of the Columbia River. No trace of the crew was ever found.
- December 11, 1900, bark *Andrada*, unknown number of dead: Disappeared off the mouth of the Columbia River and was believed to have sunk off the Washington Coast with all hands onboard.

- January 16, 1901, bark *Cape Wrath*, fifteen dead: En route from Peru, South America, to Portland. Was sighted off the mouth of the Columbia River, but neither the *Cape Wrath* nor its crew were ever seen again.
- December 1909, schooner *Susie M. Plummer*, twelve dead: Left Everett, Washington, for San Pedro in South America with a cargo of lumber. Was discovered off Cape Flattery, seemingly abandoned by its twelve-man crew. Only the *Susie M. Plummer*'s cargo kept it afloat until it washed ashore in San Josef Bay in Canada weeks later. No trace of the crew was ever found.
- February 28, 1918, schooner *Americana*, eleven dead: Cleared the Columbia River bar with a cargo of lumber, en route to Australia. No trace of the *Americana* or its crew was ever found.

Astoria, whether on land, underground or at sea, has more than its fair share of ghostly and paranormal tales.

9

MEMALOOSE

ISLANDS AND CULT OF THE DEAD

The popular Memaloose State Park is located near the Dalles in Oregon's Columbia Gorge, along the Columbia River. The Chinook Native tribe used to lay the bones of their dead on open pyres and in canoes on Memaloose Island in the middle of the Columbia River. From the 1880s until the 1930s, the Chinook burial grounds were desecrated and the dead disturbed, perhaps leaving their spirits restless.

Many Natives believed in spirits of their dead, and a spirit reappearing after death was thought to be very bad luck. Spirits frequently visited the living in dreams, begging the living to join them. To protect themselves from ghosts, Natives often buried the dead far from their villages, and many of the islands on the Columbia River were used as cemeteries. Several were called "Memaloose," based on the Chinook word *memalust*, meaning "to die." It was thought this would make it more difficult for the dead to revisit the living. Bodies were either wrapped in robes, mats or furs and left in canoes, which were placed in the woods or in grave vaults. The Natives considered these to be sacred "islands of the dead."

Lewis and Clark passed one such Memaloose on October 29, 1805, on their way to the Pacific Ocean. They called it "Sepulcher Island," meaning "burial island." On their journey back home, they visited the island on April 15, 1806. Clark described it as follows: "[We] passed three large rocks in the river, the middle rock is large, long and has several square vaults on it. We call this rocky island Sepulcher."

Photograph of a Native canoe, 1910. *Courtesy of the Library of Congress.*

One man, Victor Trevitt, a pioneer businessman and Oregon state senator from 1866 to 1874, was said to love Natives. He reportedly felt strongly connected to them and wanted to be buried near them. It is said that he told his friends, "I have but one desire after I die, to be laid away on Memaloose Island with the Indians. They are more honest than Whites and live up to the light they have. In the resurrection, I will take my chances with the Indians."

Trevitt was not without controversy, as some said he was a racist toward Black Americans. Trevitt died on January 23, 1883, and his body is said to have been placed in a snowbank on Memaloose Island until the Columbia River ice and snow melted. He was buried on Memaloose Island on March 10, 1883, with ninety Masonic members present, in a vault of stone measuring eight feet square, onto which a thirteen-foot-tall granite monument was placed. This manner of burial was notably different from the simple burial of nearby Native remains.

From 1884 to 1885, Natives were forced from their native lands and sent to reservations. Their canoe burial sites and grave vaults went uncared for. Storms, waves and vandalism added to their destruction, while the bones of the dead were bleached white by the blowing sands and sun. It is said James Hartley, a White man, looted Native graves (not Trevitt's) on Memaloose Island in the late 1800s, in search of knives, hammers, beads, arrowheads and other artifacts. He ransacked graves, tore down vaults and threw human remains onto the beach. Hartley and others like him had no care or reverence for Native remains. This lack of respect would later cost Hartley his life.

Trevitt's burial site remained untouched once again when the Bonneville Dam was constructed. Construction on the dam began in June 1934 and was finished in 1937. The resulting rising waters caused many of the Native burial islands to be covered in water. In 1937, the U.S. Army Corps of Engineers exhumed the remains of 650 Natives and moved them to a cemetery north of the Dalles Bridge. They left Trevitt's grave and monument untouched.

In addition to the islands of the dead, a Native "Ghost Cult" on the Columbia River was said to exist. It is thought that this cult was formed in reaction to the incursion of White people and the resulting deaths of 90 percent of the Chinook Natives, killed between the 1770s and 1850. Along with other coastal tribes, the Chinook Natives were killed, in part, due to diseases such as smallpox, malaria and measles. Bone carvings of human and animal figures with prominent rib cages were discovered in old burial pits, figures which the Natives believed represented death. Anthropologists have indicated there was an old Native belief in the impending destruction and renewal of the world—a belief that seemed to be confirmed by the tragic way and speed in which the Natives of the Lower Columbia Valley disappeared.

James Hartley was said to be a "collector of Indian relics and curios." He went missing in 1895, and his body was found on a small island on

Photograph of a wrecked boat, 2018. *Courtesy of ZorroP, Pixabay.*

Deadman's Lake, on the stretch from Mount Saint Helens to the Columbia River. Hartley's body had been placed in an old canoe, his hands and feet bound with rope and fastened to the canoe's stem and stern. A stake had been driven into his chest. This manner of death was said to be similar to that inflicted by Natives in the early nineteenth century.

Was Hartley killed by Natives, appropriately angry over his desecration of burial grounds, or was it the spirits whose graves Hartley desecrated that killed him? We may never know.

10

NASELLE, WASHINGTON

COLUMBIA RIVER'S ELLIS ISLAND

The small, peaceful town of Naselle was named for the Nisal Natives, a Chinook tribe that formerly lived on the Columbia River. Naselle was settled in the nineteenth century, primarily by Finnish and Scandinavian immigrants, and to this day, it cohosts a biannual "Finnish-American Folk Festival" with Astoria, Oregon. While logging remains the town's predominant industry, it may have been the United States' former policies toward ill immigrants that left the most scars on the land.

In 1891, the U.S. Congress mandated the inspection of all arriving immigrants, stipulating the exclusion of "all idiots, insane persons, paupers or persons likely to become public charges, persons suffering from a loathsome or dangerous contagious disease and criminals." On May 9, 1899, the U.S. government purchased the then-deserted Knappton Cannery for $8,000 and established the Columbia River Quarantine Station at Knappton Cove, across the Columbia River from Astoria. It was informally known as the Columbia River's "Ellis Island." It now serves as the Knappton Cove Heritage Center in Naselle, a museum with exhibits and living history reenactors. From 1899 to 1938, the center was used as one of the two federal quarantine stations north of San Francisco. Immigrants who arrived on the West Coast by ship and were suspected of carrying a contagious disease were sent to the somewhat-remote center for quarantine. These diseases included bubonic plague, yellow fever, cholera, smallpox and typhus. As described in the 1890s by Walter Wyman, the supervising surgeon general of the marine hospital service:

Photograph of immigrants, 2013. *Courtesy of Moonietunes, Pixabay.*

While the inspection of vessels at the mouth of the Columbia River is faithfully carried on, no provision is made there for the care of the sick taken from an infected vessel or the purification of the vessel itself. The nearest properly equipped quarantine station is at Diamond Point, near Port Townsend, Wash., some 275 miles distant, and should an infected vessel arrive at the mouth of the Columbia River, the vessel would have to be remanded to the Port Townsend Quarantine, entailing not only expense, but hardship upon the sick.

Some visitors to the Knappton Cove Heritage Center have reported strange occurrences, including the sighting of a woman dressed in period clothing wandering the shore. Another person swore he saw a "fiery thing" on the beach. Some paranormal investigators visited, placed a cup of coffee in one of the quarantine rooms and set up a recording device before stepping outside. When they returned, there was less coffee in the cup, and the recording device had captured the audio of someone whispering "coffee, coffee." Though documentation is limited, one could surmise that the fear of carrying a contagious disease like bubonic plague, yellow fever, cholera, smallpox and typhus, and the deaths that resulted at the center, could have caused spirits to linger there.

11

ILWACO, WASHINGTON

APPARITIONS ABOUND

What is now the pleasant fishing village of Ilwaco was once home to the Chinookan people, who fished the Columbia River. The Chinook Natives and other coastal tribes were decimated by diseases carried by White settlers, and by 1850, 90 percent of the Chinook were dead. This level of suffering and death may be one of the reasons for the many talked-about hauntings.

First called "Unity" in honor of the conclusion of the Civil War in 1865, Ilwaco was officially established in 1876 and named for the son-in-law of hereditary Chinook chief Comcoly, Elowahka Jim. A 1909 promotional brochure described Ilwaco as follows:

> *Nestling in a beautiful cove on the shores of Baker's Bay at the mouth of the Columbia River lies Ilwaco, the third largest town in Pacific County. Though but a mile from the Pacific Ocean and with the roaring surf plainly to be heard yet it is protected from the gales and storms by the wooded hills which lie between the townsite and the ocean and, but for the increased roar of the surf, no one would know of a storm at sea. The townsite is level, skirted by a low bluff, making the townsite an ideal one for building purposes.*

Ilwaco served as a transportation hub for ferry travelers from Portland and other locations, and a railway was operated by the Ilwaco Railway and Navigation Company. This "narrow gauge" (three-foot-wide) railway

Photograph of an Ilwaco, Washington wall mural. *Author's collection.*

ran for over forty years, from 1888 to 1930, from the Columbia River Bar in Ilwaco, up the Long Beach Peninsula and to Nahcotta. It had several nicknames, including the "Clamshell Railroad," the "railroad that ran with the tides" and the "Irregular, Rambling and Never-Get-There Railroad." The train carried vacationers from Portland and other passengers, mail and about eighty thousand pounds of Oysterville oysters to Ilwaco, which were, in turn, carried to Astoria and then to market in San Francisco.

One stop on the railroad was known as the "Loomis Ghost Station" and was located at the mansion of Lewis A. Loomis, the founder and president of the railway. He died in 1913, and his mansion soon fell into disrepair, described by some as a "spooky old, dilapidated house." The railroad soon ceased stopping at Loomis, and in 1953, the mansion was torn down by Loomis's son.

Ilwaco was home to fishermen and loggers, with the Cove Saloon frequented by these hardworking men and soldiers from nearby Fort Canby. Like other areas in the Graveyard of the Pacific, many shipwrecks occurred near Ilwaco, with untold numbers of dead washing ashore. Though today, fishing and tourism are popular activities, local newspapers

Photograph of an old railway, 2015. *Courtesy of Free-Photos, Pixabay.*

report that Ilwaco, like much of the area, is home to numerous apparitions and hauntings.

The Bell Tower Inn, described as charming and close to waterfront shopping, was built in 1928 as a Presbyterian church. In the 1970s and 1980s, it served as a barracks for fishermen before being converted into a bed-and-breakfast. Witnesses have reported hearing the sounds of disembodied footsteps and strange, unexplainable noises, as well as seeing curtains raising themselves.

The Ilwaco Community Building, used for various events, was originally a hospital. Witnesses have reported seeing the ghosts of children, as well as ghostly orbs of energy, within the building. Some have reported seeing, through a front window, a man's apparition holding a baby near the area that was once the maternity ward. The spirit of a red-haired woman has been spotted walking toward what used to be a patient's room, papers have been known to rustle and move on their own and disembodied footsteps and knocking have been heard.

Spirits have likewise been reported at the modern Ocean Beach Hospital next door, which took on the role of the former hospital. One witness, a night nurse, was making her rounds when, by the surgical ward, she saw a white-robed spirit moving down the hall with no visible legs. The figure then vanished. Another witness reported that while trying to settle his wife in for treatment at the hospital, he witnessed a female apparition walking across the room and passing through the table, before exiting through the wall.

12

CAPE DISAPPOINTMENT

DEADMANS HOLLOW AND NOT RESTING IN PEACE

C ape Disappointment is a state park and headland located next to Ilwaco. Here, you will find dramatic scenery, cliffs, beaches and forests. It was named in 1788 by Captain John Meares, who was looking for shelter for his ship from the violent seas. Meares was searching for the entrance to the Columbia River but was left "disappointed" when he could not find it. In its 2019 four-part series on the Graveyard of the Pacific, the Travel Channel's *Ghost Adventures* program focused on Cape Disappointment. They found numerous unexplained paranormal phenomena.

Because of the treacherous waters surrounding the cape, the coast guard station located close by is the largest search-and-rescue operation on the Northwest Coast, with as many as two hundred yearly calls for assistance. It was at Cape Disappointment that Lewis, Clark and the Corps of Discovery ended their expedition in 1805. The year 1853 was particularly disastrous for shipwrecks in the mouth of the Columbia River. Three "barks"—large, three-masted sailing ships—sunk that year. One was the *Oriole*, which was carrying supplies to build a lighthouse. Another was the *Vandalia*, which sunk on January 9, 1853. Its hull was found bottom up on the beach near the mouth of the Columbia River several days later. It was thought that it wandered into the treacherous breakers, sprung a leak, then sunk, with all twelve crew members lost. Four bodies washed ashore: Captain E.N. Beard, for whom Beards Hollow was named, and three other crew washed into what is now known as Deadmans Hollow. One could speculate that the spirits of these dead sailors may still linger at

Photograph of North Head Lighthouse, Ilwaco, Washington. *Author's collection.*

Cape Disappointment, in Beards and Deadmans Hollows, trapped by the swift currents and treacherous waters.

The U.S. government built navigational lights at the cape in the late 1850s, prompted by the thousands of shipwrecks and unknown lives lost. The U.S. Life-Saving Service (precursor to the coast guard) established stations at the cape beginning in 1877, and by 1894, a five-mile-long jetty was created to partially stabilize the shifting sandbar. The jetty was extended in 1914, and another was completed in 1925. More lights were added, and lightships were anchored along the coast beginning in 1898.

Cape Disappointment Lighthouse and North Head Lighthouse stand near the Cape. The North Head was put into service on May 16, 1898, and it still serves as an active navigational aid, though lighthouse keepers have since been replaced by an automated beacon. Life for the lighthouse keepers was harsh. They had few visitors and kept a strict twenty-four-hour schedule to tend the flame that helped ships navigate the graveyard. Adding to the harshness, the lighthouse is located at the second-windiest lighthouse site in the United States, experiencing winds up to 120 miles per hour.

Photograph of North Head Lighthouse grounds, Ilwaco, Washington. *Author's collection.*

It was this hard life that is believed to have driven the wife of the first lighthouse keeper over the steep cliffs in 1923. Alexander K. Pesonen, nicknamed "A.K." and "Ikey," arrived at the North Head Lighthouse in 1888. He married Mary Watson (born 1870), nicknamed "Soney," in 1890. Only twenty years old at the start, Mary endured this lonely, difficult life and the howling winds for twenty-five years. In the spring of 1923, Keeper Pesonen took Mary to a doctor in Portland. It was reported that she was diagnosed with "melancholia, with persistent depression and ill-founded fears."

The couple returned to North Head on June 8, and the next morning, Mary rose early and went for a walk with her dog Jerry. It was reported that Jerry returned a short time later, acting strangely. A search party found Mary's coat lying on the edge of a cliff, 194 feet above the churning ocean. The tall grass leading to the cliff was disturbed, as if someone had slid down the cliff. At great personal risk, Second Assistant Lighthouse Keeper Frank C. Hammond located and secured Mary's body from a cove at the base of the cliff. Mary had been a member of the "Unity Movement," known for faith-based healings. A letter was discovered, which she reportedly wrote the night before her suicide. In the letter, she stated, "I see where I have been wrong in a great many ways, but please, God, I will try and change and do better….I'm even going to try and do without my medicine and just pray I'll get better and better."

Her death occurred just six months before her husband's planned retirement, which was to take place on September 30, 1923. They had intended to buy a cranberry farm just a few miles away and spend their winters in California. Instead, Mary's body was buried in the Ilwaco Cemetery, as was her husband's, who died two years later. Several newspapers reported on Mary's "rash act, illness, and temporary insanity," which caused "a troubled Mary to finally escape the harsh environment that had driven her mad." Beginning in the 1950s, and to this day, groundskeepers, volunteers and visitors have reported seeing Mary's ghost wandering through the lighthouse and the house where she and Alexander lived, appearing sad and distraught. It is thought that Mary is not resting in peace.

13

SEAVIEW, WASHINGTON

HAUNTED HOSTELS

Seaview was founded in 1880 by Jonathan Stout, a cooper (someone who made or repaired wooden casks and barrels) from Ohio. He called the area Stout's, Ocean View and North Pacific Beach before finally settling on the name Seaview. Seaview became a stop on the Clamshell Railroad and should be a stop on your road trip, as several haunted locations have been identified there.

The elegant, charming and historic fifteen-room Shelburne Hotel, built in 1896, is the longest continuously operating hotel in Washington State. Built by Charles Beaver and named after a grand hotel in Dublin, Ireland, the Shelburne was once a stop on the Clamshell Railroad. After breaking his arm during construction, Beaver was physically limited, and his wife and daughter had to handle many of his hotelier duties until he sold the Shelburne fifteen years later. According to local legend, the workload that Mr. Beaver unintentionally placed on his family deeply upset him, and it is said that is why he haunts the Shelburne to this day. His ghost has reportedly been seen walking the halls, possibly in search of something in need of repair. The sound of knocking is said to come from some of the rooms, strange temperature changes occur and the doors to empty rooms sometimes become locked from the inside. It was reported that once, in the hotel's bar, a man began acting so strangely that some thought he was possessed by one of the hotel's spirits. Appropriately, the Shelburne Hotel holds a "Spirit Gathering" just before Halloween, with "ghost themed cocktails, spooky foods," tarot card readings, self-led ghost tours and a scary movie.

Photograph of the Shelburne Inn, Seaview, Washington. *Author's collection.*

At Rod's Lamplighter Restaurant and Lounge (which is said to have excellent clam chowder), staff and patrons have described seeing a ghost named Katherine. Katherine reportedly wears a long white dress with puffy sleeves and a high collar and can be seen in the women's bathroom. Legend states that Katherine was murdered by her lover, a sea captain, and thrown in the cistern (a receptacle to catch rainwater). It has also been reported that a male ghost dressed in a black coat walks through the bar. It is thought this could be the spirit of Louie Sloan, a deceased former owner whose ashes are on display in the restaurant. It is said that lights flicker on and off, billiard balls roll by themselves and disembodied footsteps can be heard. One woman reported feeling a hand brush over her face and through her hair. Kitchen staff have reported pots and utensils swinging by themselves, and they sometimes catch a glimpse of someone out of the corner of their eye, but when they look, no one is there. It was reported that the second story was destroyed by a fire sometime in the late 1800s, killing two children; it has been said that their light footsteps can still be heard.

The serene Lions Paw Inn, built in 1911, was the first hospital on the Long Beach Peninsula. Numerous reported paranormal sightings and occurrences suggest some spirits may linger in the former hospital's halls. One such report describes a nurse-like figure who enters hotel rooms early in the morning, as if checking on hospital patients. Others reported seeing a woman in the upstairs guestroom, called the French Quarter, gazing sadly out the window. In other reports, guests tell of smelling an overwhelming scent of bacon cooking between the hours of 3:00 and 4:00 a.m. And on another occasion, three ghostly apparitions in early twentieth-century clothing were observed playing croquet on the lawn. If you visit the Lion's Paw Inn, be sure to have your croquet mallet on hand, as you may just be invited to join a ghostly game.

14

LONG BEACH, WASHINGTON

HAUNTED LAKE, HOTELS AND LEWIS AND CLARK'S LEGACIES

L ong Beach was originally founded in 1880 as "Tinkerville" by Henry Harrison Tinker; it was a stop on the Clamshell Railroad from 1889 until 1930. The boardwalk near the railroad station was called "Rubberneck Row," as pedestrians would turn to see the incoming and outgoing train. The city didn't become Long Beach until January 18, 1922. In addition to the fun "by-the-sea" atmosphere and excellent restaurants, Long Beach's list of hauntings, though not long, is intriguing.

There is a tiny lake located half a mile from Long Beach, not surprisingly called "Tinker Lake," after Henry Harrison Tinker. You can fish for largemouth bass and yellow perch in the eleven-acre, six-foot-deep lake. But legend has it that something else is present—the ghost of a man who was killed there many years ago and thrown into the lake. The killer was never caught, and when the victim's body was found, all that remained was bones. One witness reported seeing a phantom at the lake at sunrise. He said the spirit appeared for a moment, then vanished.

The fifty-year-old rustic Lighthouse Oceanfront Resort is reputed to have at least two resident ghosts in rooms 101 and 105. Guests have reported furniture rearranging itself, TVs turning on and off, rocking chairs rocking by themselves and the sounds of ghostly whispers. Likewise, the cozy Thunderbird Motel, which is walking distance from the beach, is said to be haunted by a "disturbed" spirit who is known to play with the electricity. In 2005, a guest reported that a radio stopped playing music, only to be replaced with a scratching, static sound, as well as the lights flickering and

Photograph of a Long Beach, Washington wall mural. *Author's collection.*

going out. At the same time, the guest reported that it became so cold in the room that she and her husband could see their breath. At 3:00 a.m., the guest was awakened by the bedroom doorknob rattling and the door opening on its own before slamming shut with great force.

Explorer Merriweather Lewis, one half of the Corps of Discovery that explored the West and is noted for visiting this area, died a mysterious and untimely death. There are numerous parks, forts, statues and plaques in the Long Beach and Astoria areas commemorating the visit. After the expedition, Lewis became governor of the Louisiana Territory. On October 10, 1809, on his way from Louisiana to Washington, D.C., Lewis stayed at the Grinder's Stand Inn near Hohenwald, Tennessee. Mrs. Grinder observed Lewis "pacing and mumbling in a strange manner." Later that night, after Lewis had gone to bed, it is said that Mrs. Grinder was awakened by two gunshots, and through a crack in her bedroom door, she saw Lewis stagger and fall, followed by him exclaiming, "Oh, Lord," as he crawled down the hall. Mrs. Grinder didn't summon Lewis's servants until two hours after he was shot. They discovered him lying on a blood-soaked robe, with gunshot wounds in his side and head. Lewis told them he was "no coward, but was strong," and said it was "so hard to die."

Above: Photograph of a Long Beach, Washington lake. *Author's collection.*

Left: Photograph of the Lighthouse Oceanfront Resort, Long Beach, Washington. *Author's collection.*

Left: Photograph of an old fort, 2018. *Courtesy of MikeGoad, Pixabay.*

Below: Photograph of a vintage park sign. *Author's collection.*

Lewis & Clark End of Trail

He was buried on the inn's property, which is part of today's Meriwether Lewis State Park and is commemorated by the Meriwether Lewis National Monument. The historic marker mentions the controversy surrounding Lewis's death: "Life of romantic endeavor and lasting achievement came tragically and mysteriously to its close." To this day, it is unclear if Lewis's death was a suicide or murder. Visitors to the monument have reported feeling a restless energy and a strange force pervading the isolated spot. Visitors have also reported hearing metal, like a water scoop, scraping an empty bucket, as well as the words "so hard to die." The visitors are left wondering if Meriwether Lewis is trying to set the record straight about his death.

Next time you visit one of the sites commemorating Lewis and Clark's visit to this area, contemplate Lewis's fate, the reports of his ghost, and listen for any strange sounds and voices. Perhaps Tennessee is not the only place where Lewis's ghost lingers.

15

OCEAN PARK, WASHINGTON

"THE WRECKAGE"

The peaceful town of Ocean Park was established in 1883 as a Methodist camp. The oldest continuing retail business in Washington State, Jack's Country Store, was founded here in 1885. It was a stop on the Clamshell Railroad from 1889 to 1930. Ocean Park is worth a stop if you're looking for the paranormal.

The Wreckage is a log house made of tongue-and-groove lumber that was thrown overboard by the steamer *Washington* as it narrowly avoided being wrecked in the Graveyard of the Pacific. Cement for the foundation was obtained from the French bark *Alice*, a three-masted, steel, square-rigged ship built in 1901, that was carrying a cargo of cement when it wrecked just off the Ocean Park Coast in 1909, remaining eerily upright with masts and tattered sails visible above the water. The *Alice* looked like a ghost ship rising from the waves.

The house was built by author Guy S. Allison in 1912, who also created a "zoo" of driftwood animal shapes surrounding the house, called the "Wreckage Park Zoo," which was featured in *Ripley's Believe It or Not*. The zoo animals gradually disappeared over the years, as did several outbuildings. Did they disappear due to mischievous teenagers, or was it related to the fate of the wrecked *Alice*?

Ocean Park has other reported supernatural activity. One witness described looking at an apartment with her daughter. When she opened the upstairs bedroom door, a black dog was sitting there. They shut the door, then opened it a moment later. The dog was gone, but a lady in

Photograph of "The Wreckage," Ocean Park, Washington. *Author's collection.*

nineteenth-century clothing, wearing a long white apron and white hat or bonnet, had appeared. She was carrying a casserole dish. They again shut the door and immediately left the apartment. The witness knew she and her daughter were the only people there, as they had the key and the door had been locked.

Another witness described regularly walking through the Surfside area of Ocean Park. He would cross through a cranberry bog behind T Lane on a road that was used by service vehicles. He said that each time he traveled through the area, he experienced the same eerie feeling. On one such occasion, he saw red eyes in the bush following him, but he was certain it wasn't a bear, elk or deer. That was the last time he took that path. There appears to be no logical explanation for the eerie feeling and red eyes. Could something paranormal be the explanation?

16

OYSTERVILLE, WASHINGTON

"AND THE SEA GAVE UP THE DEAD"

The Chinook Natives gathered oysters in nearby Willapa Bay for centuries. The town, named for the rich oyster beds, was established in 1854 by J.A. Clark. From 1880 to 1890, Oysterville was a busy port, transporting the lucrative and plentiful oysters harvested there. It had two deep-water wharves, churches, schools, canneries and other businesses, and the town prospered. Oysterville became the county seat and held this title until "raiders" from South Bend, Washington, ransacked the courthouse and stole important papers, making South Bend the county seat. There is a large plaque in town reflecting this series of events. The theft, depletion of the oyster beds and purported hauntings caused Oysterville to become a literal ghost town.

Today, Oysterville is a beautiful and serene village at the northern tip of the Long Beach Peninsula. Visiting the town is like stepping back in time. It is home to a historic cemetery, numerous nineteenth-century houses, a church and a one-room schoolhouse—all with plaques describing their histories. The town is listed in the National Register of Historic Places, and some of the descendants of the original settlers still live here. Not surprisingly, haunted tales abound.

Oysterville has one of the oldest cemeteries in Washington State, dating back to 1858. It is located a quarter of a mile outside the historic boomtown. The two-acre cemetery holds the graves of several of the founders of the area, including those of the Espy and Clark families. Its tombstones also contain the hidden histories of the early pioneers and Natives, as do the

Photograph of an Oysterville, Washington sign. *Author's collection.*

unmarked graves of sailors and shipwreck passengers whose bodies washed ashore in the Graveyard of the Pacific.

There is a memorial to the last Native chieftain, Chief Nahcati of the Chinook, of the Long Beach Peninsula. Chief Nahcati befriended one of Oysterville's cofounders, R.H. Espy (born 1826, died 1918), and he showed him the nearby oyster beds. The village Nahcotta, three miles to the south, is named for the chief. The cemetery is reputed to either sit on top of or next to a Native burial ground, though it isn't clear if this is true.

The belief in haunted Native burial grounds is long-standing. In America, the revolutionary poet Philip Freneau believed these locations were mystical, sacred and filled with spirits that were still hunting, feasting and playing. Freneau wrote in his 1787 poem titled "The Indian Burying Ground":

> *Thou, stranger, that shalt come this way,*
> *No fraud upon the dead commit—*
> *Observe the swelling turf, and say*
> *They do not lie, but here they sit.*

Photograph of the Oysterville, Washington cemetery. *Author's collection.*

The last Native princess of the area, Myrtle Jane Johnson Woodcock (the great-granddaughter of both Chief Uhlahnee of the Chinooks and Chief Hoqueem of the Quinault tribe), is buried in Oysterville Cemetery's plot 67. When she was born, the chiefs of several tribes arrived in canoes to celebrate.

Photograph of the Oysterville, Washington cemetery. *Author's collection.*

In addition, there is a wooden sign with a marble headstone that honors the unknown sailors who were lost at sea and buried in Oysterville Cemetery, with a plaque stating the beginning of Revelations 20:13, "And the sea gave up the dead."

There are numerous drowning victims buried in Oysterville Cemetery, including:

- James R. Johnson (born 1848, died 1889), lost at sea;
- Julius Mac (born 1873, died 1918), drowned in Shoalwater Bay;
- Frank A. Rusk (born 1876, died 1900), drowned;
- John W. Smith (born 1903, died 1947), lifeguard at Ilwaco, drowned;
- A.T. Stream (born 1846, died 1916), captain, lost at sea;
- Thomas W. Stream (born 1882, died 1914), lost at sea;
- Carl A. Tanger (born 1829, died 1873), drowned in Shoalwater Bay;
- Mr. Cline, drowned in 1863 with W.B. Wells (presumed to be buried here, too).

Oysterville's original schoolhouse was a "little red schoolhouse" built in 1863. The booming town required a bigger school, and a two-story building was built and used until 1905, when it burned down. School was held elsewhere until 1907, when the current one-story replacement building was built. It served the community until 1957 and is currently a meeting place (children attend schools in Ocean Park, Long Beach and Ilwaco). The schoolhouse is also said to be haunted by the ghost of a child who died from an epileptic seizure.

Given its history, first as a booming town then as a struggling ghost town; a cemetery that reportedly sits atop an old Native burial ground; and the many drowning victims buried here, it's no surprise that ghost stories abound. As evidenced by the previous stops on our road trip, towns that have experienced calamitous events or are the final resting places of people who have experienced tragic deaths are said to have high levels of paranormal activity. Unexplained cold spots, drafts and strange energy have been reported there.

17

TOKELAND, WASHINGTON

HAUNTED HOTEL

The town of Tokeland was named for Chief Toke of the Shoalwater Bay tribe, who lived in the region in the late eighteenth century. George Brown established Tokeland in 1858, and his daughter Lizzie and her husband built the Kindred Inn (later renamed the Tokeland Hotel) in 1885. In 1910, Portland, Oregon investors sought to develop a Coney Island–type amusement park in Tokeland, though this plan never came to fruition. There is nothing Coney Island–like about the hotel's purported active apparitions.

The lovely and welcoming Tokeland Hotel is the oldest in Washington State. It is in the National Register of Historic Places and is said to be haunted by a ghost named "Charley." The story goes that Charley was a Chinese immigrant who was illegally smuggled into the United States from China to work on the railroads. The fireplace at the Tokeland Hotel has a secret space behind it, in which illegal immigrants hid to avoid detection. In the 1930s, while hiding behind the chimney, Charley reportedly suffocated. His ghost has been seen in the hallways, and dinner plates are known to fly across the room.

One witness, an author who was writing an article for a website, described touring the hotel with the owner. He said that when they returned to the third-floor stairway to go back to the second floor, they encountered a flickering lightbulb at the top of the stairs. The author noted that neither he, the owner nor the hotel staff had turned on the light. He also relayed how guests who were staying in the second-floor rooms claimed to hear noises above them late at night that sounded like someone sliding coat hangers. However, the third floor was never used for accommodations, only storage.

The author also described the hotel owner's experiences. He said the owner was working on the second floor when she noticed a floating, foggy apparition that was a few feet tall and one and a half feet off the ground. The apparition floated in the middle of the hallway, looking similar to a cumulus cloud. Another time, the owner was retrieving an article from a storeroom on the first floor. The door to the room closed behind her, and she heard the latch being thrown; she was locked in the dark room. She grabbed a piece of wood and pounded on the door to get someone's attention. However, the storeroom was in a part of the hotel that was far from the areas used by guests and staff. She turned on her flashlight, but it immediately turned off. The owner felt her way to the light switch several feet from the door, but the light wouldn't turn on. She went back to the door with the intention of pounding again but found it unlocked.

On another occasion, while doing minor repairs in the hotel, the author says the owner narrowly missed being struck in the head by a very heavy, old metal roller skate, which fell from the top shelf of a bookcase. Alarmed, she checked to make sure the bookcase was solidly placed against the wall—it was. She grabbed the top shelf and tried to move the bookcase, but it was sturdy and wouldn't budge. Finally, she checked to see if the top shelf was sloped but found it was perfectly level. The hotel was empty, and there was no logical explanation for this event.

The owner also detailed to the website author her late husband's haunted experiences. Her husband told of a fisherman who swore his lunch plate lifted off the table, spun around and set itself back down again, leaving the fisherman "weirded out." He also told of seeing a bright, gleaming white glow on the kitchen floor. He said it looked like direct sunlight from a window, but when he put his hand over it, it did not create a shadow. A staff member came into the kitchen and saw the same thing before the light quickly disappeared.

The hotel is also said to be home to the ghost of a cat that wanders around the building. Room 7, the purported site of a long-ago murder, is said to be the most haunted location in the hotel.

18

Aberdeen, Cosmopolis, Hoquiam and Moclips, Washington

Ghoul of Grays Harbor, Haunted Museums and a Ghost Forest

Aberdeen Apparitions

Aberdeen, a hardworking, seafaring town, was founded in 1884 by Samuel Benn. By the late nineteenth century, the town was home to thirty-seven major sawmills. It was also the hotbed of many shady activities, including wild saloons, gambling and brothels, earning it the nickname the "Hellhole of the Pacific." Another nickname it had was the "Port of Missing Men," reflecting the disappearances and murders of several sailors and others who were passing through.

Billy Gohl nicknamed the "Ghoul of Grays Harbor" and the "Timber Town Killer," resided in Aberdeen in the late nineteenth and early twentieth centuries. Gohl may have been the worst—yet least remembered—serial killer in American history, believed to have murdered well over one hundred men, though he was only convicted for two.

An imposing figure at six feet, two inches tall and powerfully built, the German-born Gohl had failed as a gold prospector in the Yukon. He worked for a time in San Francisco's wharves before working as a bartender. In 1903, Gohl moved to Aberdeen, where he worked as an official for the Sailor's Union of the Pacific (SUP). It was in this role that Gohl was accused, in 1906, of attempting to "shanghai" nonunion crewmen from the schooner *Fearless*. Gohl reportedly arrived with a gang of armed men and fired his Colt at the ship's captain. Though a crew member was killed, the SUP got the charges dropped, and Gohl was fined $1,250.

Photograph of a gun, 2017. *Courtesy of Monoar-CGI-Artist, Pixabay.*

About a year after Gohl's arrival in Aberdeen, the number of "floaters" (lifeless bodies found floating in the water) dramatically increased around the Wishkah River and Grays Harbor. Townsfolk referred to the bodies as the "Floater Fleet." The SUP building served as the center for Gohl's unsavory activities. Sailors, new to the area, would inevitably visit the union in search of a job or, if they were already a member, to take care of personal business. Gohl would inquire whether the sailors had family or friends in the area. The topic would then shift to that of money and belongings. If the sailor had items to steal and they wouldn't be missed by family or friends, Gohl would make them his next murder victim. Gohl's preferred method of murder was shooting, but poisoning, strangling and bludgeoning were also employed. He would dispose of the corpses in the Wishkah River, which ran behind the union hall and into Grays Harbor. Some say Gohl used a trapdoor and chute to carry his victims to the river.

Gohl was arrested in February 1910 and admitted his guilt. He claimed there was no trapdoor where one was thought to be and said that if there had been one, it would only open into the saloon, not the river. Gohl recounted what he would do if a sailor came into the SUP office and gave Gohl personal belongings, including money, to store for him. Gohl would tell the sailor that a "scab" boat was coming in and that the sailor should dress in a logger's outfit to wait on a piling at the dock for the boat. Gohl would then get his rifle, aim through his office's window and shoot the sailor in the head.

One of Gohl's accomplices, John Klingenberg, confirmed Gohl's guilt in exchange for leniency by the court. Klingenberg testified that Gohl had met with sailor Charles Hatberg on December 21, 1909, whose lifeless body was discovered on February 2, 1910. Hatberg had been murdered with a .28 pistol owned by Gohl. Gohl told a barkeep at the Grand Saloon that he wouldn't be seeing Hatberg again, saying: "You won't. He's sleeping off Indian Creek with an anchor for a pillow." Hatberg's body was found not far

Photograph of Aberdeen, Washington, 1911. *Courtesy of the Library of Congress.*

from shore, weighed down by a twenty-five-pound anchor. Gohl later denied everything, proclaiming "It's a frame-up." Inexplicably, many believed him. Klingenberg also said he witnessed Gohl "sit on John Hoffman's chest and shoot him in the forehead, despite him begging for his life." They then threw Hoffman's lifeless body overboard.

When brought to trial, Gohl claimed Hatberg and Hoffman were in Alaska, working as lighthouse keepers. The prosecutor brought Hatberg's arm, which had been preserved, into court so jurors could examine identifying tattoos. In speaking about Hoffman and Hatberg, Gohl is reported to have said: "They went away for good." Gohl was found guilty, though the jury spared him from the death penalty by requesting leniency. He was found guilty on May 12, 1910, and sentenced to two consecutive life terms at the Walla Walla State Penitentiary. In exchange for his cooperation, Klingenberg was sentenced to twenty years in prison. Several human skulls were later found near Gohl's cabin.

Gohl was later moved to the Eastern State Psychiatric Hospital in Spokane County, Washington. It was established in 1891 and remains in operation. It was said Gohl went insane due to either a stabbing he witnessed in prison or complications from syphilis. He died in the asylum in 1927. Gohl is buried in Eastern State Psychiatric Hospital's Cemetery No. 1 in an unmarked grave. There are at least 4,440 unmarked and mixed gravesites there, and some of the remains have been reburied several times. With Gohl's resting place there, it is best not to visit at night.

In modern-day Aberdeen, Billy's Bar & Grill at the corner of East Heron and South G Streets is known for its fun environment and excellent food. Named after the serial killer, the pub also contains nostalgia from Aberdeen's past. Some in Aberdeen believe Gohl's spirit and the spirits of his victims wander in and around the restaurant. The sights and sounds of lights turning on and off, disembodied voices and sailors in early twentieth-century clothing, as well as the feeling of cold spots, are commonplace. Drinking

glasses have been seen flying through the air before smashing against the wall. A Billy's employee is said to have seen a man resembling Gohl sitting at the bar late one night, staring at her before vanishing. In the pub's upstairs area, ghosts of prostitutes and Gohl's victims are said to linger.

If you find yourself in Aberdeen, Washington, be sure to drop by Billy's. It may be more than food and drink that you experience. While visiting Aberdeen, be sure to also see the *Lady Washington* sailing ship. It is a replica of Captain Robert Gray's (Grays Harbor is named for him) 1788 ship. It was used as the HMS *Interceptor*—the fastest warship in the British Royal fleet—in the *Pirates of the Caribbean* movie franchise. Although there are no stories of it being haunted, it adds to the haunted ambience of the Aberdeen area.

COSMOPOLIS CREEPINGS

There are said to be several other haunted locations in the Aberdeen area. In Cosmopolis, a peaceful small town incorporated in 1891, the historic Cooney Mansion Bed and Breakfast (B&B) was built in 1908. Set on top of a lovely, scenic hill, the bed-and-breakfast, nicknamed the "Spruce Cottage," was the home of lumber baron Neil Cooney, who never married. It is said the bed-and-breakfast is haunted by no fewer than seven ghosts. Disembodied voices, footsteps behind guests, touching of hair, images in mirrors, cold spots and the unexplained closing of doors and room lockouts have been known to occur. Unexplained electromagnetic fields have also been detected, possibly indicating a ghostly presence.

The lumber city of Hoquiam, incorporated in 1890, has its own tales of hauntings. The fascinating Polson Museum, built in 1924 as a colonial mansion, is said to be haunted by a female spirit dressed in white, as well as the spirit of a young child in the nursery.

GHOST FOREST

In Moclips (a Native word for "large stream"), the Museum of North Beach, described as "incredible," has been said to be the site of numerous unexplained paranormal events. Ghostly voices and strange music have been heard in the museum. These spirits may be those of a mill employee who was hit by a passing train, a blind woman who died in a house fire, a fireman and engineer who were crushed by a falling tree and numerous shipwreck victims.

South of Moclips, on the coast, lies a very strange and otherworldly sight. The Copalis Ghost Forest is a forest of dead red cedar and spruce trees, a consequence of the massive 9.0-magnitude earthquake and resulting tsunami that rocked the Washington Coast on the evening of January 26, 1700. As a result of the tsunami, the land instantly sank six feet, and the forest was flooded by saltwater.

The Makah tribe tells of the huge 1700 earthquake, which happened in the middle of the night. Those who followed their elder's advice to run for high ground survived. After spending a cold night in the hills with animals that had also fled the rushing waters, the survivors found that the former coastal villages had been completely washed away or buried under mudslides, leaving no survivors.

The forest is amazing and eerie at the same time. It consists of 320-year-old dead tree trunks standing in a low grassy area by the water.

19

LA PUSH AND FORKS, WASHINGTON

GHOSTS, WEREWOLVES, SASQUATCH, SEVERED FEET AND SHIPWRECKS

APPARITIONS

Sitting at the mouth of the Quillayute River, La Push is a small, scenic coastal village within the Quileute Native Reservation in Northwestern Washington. Like many of the small towns we have explored along the often fog-shrouded coast, La Push has its fair share of haunted history.

The La Push area, particularly its Native population, has experienced terrible calamities over the years. In 1701, smallpox decimated about 30 percent of the Native population. It is estimated the epidemic killed more than eleven thousand Natives in Western Washington, reducing the population from approximately thirty-seven thousand to twenty-six thousand.

Tragedy soon struck again. As described by an elderly Squamish Native man in the 1890s, misfortune befell his people when locally caught salmon were found to be covered in sores and blotches and unfit for consumption. However, because his people depended on the fish, they continued to catch and store the salmon for the winter's food supply. Though they put off eating the salmon for as long as possible, they eventually ate the fish. The Natives became very sick as a horrible skin disease broke out; none were spared. Men, women and children died in agony by the hundreds. When spring arrived and fresh food was finally available, there were hardly any Natives left. It was reported that the level of mortality was so great, it was impossible for the survivors to bury their dead. Rather, they simply pulled the houses down over the bodies and left them there.

As we have seen, tragedies like those just described tend to be associated with increased paranormal activity. These types of disasters scar the land and the environment. Possibly related to these tragedies, ghostly apparitions are said to walk along the beach, including one of a little boy that is said to disappear when approached. Could it be that these ghostly sightings are related to the historical events and tragedies that were experienced there?

VAMPIRES AND WEREWOLVES

Forks is probably best known as the town at the center of the *Twilight* saga, the bestselling vampire and werewolf book series and extremely successful movie franchise. It's a cute town located in a foggy, forested setting often described as "spooky." The Quileute tribe depicted in the movies actually exists in this area, with their reservation located alongside La Push.

The Quileute origin story describes K'wati, a "shape shifter," who turned a pair of wolves into humans. In folklore and mythology, shapeshifting is the supernatural ability to physically transform from one form to another. Two creatures characterized as having the ability to shapeshift are werewolves and vampires. Shapeshifting into a wolf is called lycanthropy, and the belief in werewolves (Old English for "man-wolf") and lycanthropes (Greek for "wolf-person") is widespread. Depending on the culture, there are differing ways in which individuals are said to be able to transform. These methods are said to include drinking certain substances, witchcraft and entering satanic agreements. Likewise, cultures differ on how the condition can be corrected or ended, though some suggested methods are

Photograph of a wolf.
Courtesy of Pixabay.

"wolfsbane," a poisonous plant said to fight against supernatural creatures; surgery; exorcism; and being killed by a silver bullet.

The Quileutes believe their tribe is descended from wolves and belongs to a "wolf society," which holds ceremonies celebrating the tribe's ancestry and origin story. Such ceremonies are said to involve a rhythmic wolf dance and the wearing of wolf head–shaped headdresses. Quileute culture includes several mythological creatures; in addition to K'wati the shape shifter, there is the thunderbird that is powerful enough to carry a whale in its claws and the Dask'iya or cannibal ogress. *Twilight* author Stephenie Meyer credited the Quileutes' beliefs with inspiring the werewolf characters in her series. She chose Forks as the primary setting in her books after looking up the rainiest locations in America and visiting the town.

Sasquatch

In the Pacific Northwest, legends of Sasquatch and Bigfoot abound. Some people swear they've seen and heard these large ape-like creatures. In part, the origin of the Bigfoot is tied to Native and European folklore surrounding the "wild man" figure.

Natives strongly believed the Sasquatch was real. There are ancient tales of "wild men" who lurked near villages and left immense footprints. Members of the Plateau tribes, such as those at the Warm Springs Reservation in North-Central Oregon, described Sasquatch as a "stick Indian," potentially hostile beings who stole salmon and confused people by whistling, causing them to become lost. As documented in 1865 by ethnographer George Gibbs, Pacific Northwest Natives described the "Tsiatko," hirsute "wild Indians" of the woods. Natives told tales of these large, wild and hairy men. In 1898, Chief Mischelle of the Nlaka'pamux in British Columbia told the story of a creature he called "the benign-faced-one." Members of the Lummi tell tales of "Ts'emekwes," while other tribes use different names, including "stiyaha," "kwi-kwiyai" and "skoocooms." Though most tales describe benign giants living among the people and stealing salmon from fishing nets, others describe dangerous and even cannibalistic creatures. According to a nineteenth-century legend, children were warned against saying the names of these creatures for fear that the beings would hear them and carry off or kill someone. To this day, tales of these beings are still told on reservations.

The Pacific Northwest is home to a significant number of proud Americans of Finnish descent, and their stories may have contributed to the Sasquatch legend. One Finnish mythical creature that is said to be found in the woods is called the "Peikko." The Peikko is reported to be a slow, large, hairy, wild ape-like creature. Some are said to be aggressive, and they are thought to be related to trolls, giants and goblins. It could be that the legend of the Peikko, brought to America by immigrating Finns, added to Sasquatch sightings in the Pacific Northwest.

Sasquatch (or Bigfoot) began capturing the public's attention when it was first widely described in the Oregon area in 1904. Sightings of these hairy wild men were reported by settlers in the Coastal Range, with similar accounts spread by miners and hunters in later decades. In 1924, miners on Mount St. Helens claimed to have been attacked by giant "apes" in an incident that was widely reported in Oregon newspapers. Around 1958, loggers to the east and west of the Cascade Mountains began reporting sightings of Sasquatch-like creatures and discovering their immense tracks along logging roads. Witnesses observed these beings crossing roads at night, striding furtively through forest and mountain terrain and digging for and eating ground squirrels in rock piles.

In 1970, Peter Byrne established the "Bigfoot Information Center" at the Dalles along the Columbia River, which featured documented eyewitness testimony and footprints.

HAUNTED GRAVEYARD

Another area legend isn't about vampires or werewolves—it's about a haunted graveyard. Beaver Hill, a popular hiking and camping site not far from Forks, is the site of the reputed and long-forgotten "Tragedy" Graveyard. The events that gave rise to the legend involve an individual named Charley Paul, who lived in a homestead near Forks in the late 1890s. Charley, who was reported to have been missing an eye and never seen smiling, lived across Lake Pleasant from Rose and Charles Brenton. According to legend, Charley fell in love with Rose, and while she was away from home visiting family, he killed Charles and made it look like a suicide. Inexplicably, Rose is said to have soon become "taken up" with a man named Paul. After Paul left to work in Port Angeles, Rose reportedly took up with a man named Dave McKunckle. Charley ambushed McKunckle and shot him dead. After a violent fight, Charley reportedly murdered Rose before committing suicide. All were buried on Beaver Hill.

According to legend, others who experienced violent deaths are buried in the graveyard. These individuals include a man named Joe Neederstrauser, who shot his mining business partner before shooting himself; and a man named Winkler, who went mad and died when he got lost in the woods. The last person buried here was a man named Terwilliger, who suffered from an illness and committed suicide in 1906.

Is the legend of Tragedy Graveyard real, and is this graveyard really the final resting place of so many who experienced tragic, violent deaths? Though we will probably never know, the area is said to be haunted by the ghosts of those who died violent and strange deaths.

Severed Feet

Speaking of odd occurrences, severed feet keep washing ashore along the coasts of Northern Washington and Southern BC. These severed feet are found still in sneakers, hiking boots and other shoes. Some of the shoe brands that have been found include three New Balance, two Nike and an Ozark Trail.

Since 2007, sixteen of these detached human feet have been found in Washington and BC. Most of them are right feet. At least one discovered foot was analyzed by the BC Coroners Service. They couldn't tell how long the foot had been in the water, but the regional coroner said the model of shoe had gone on the market after March 2013. The coroner is working with local police to see if any reported disappearances are connected to the discovery.

In 2007, the first two feet—both right feet—were found in BC just six days apart. The Royal Canadian Mounted Police said that finding them in such a short timeframe was suspicious. In 2008, another five feet were found, including in Washington. Speculation about the origins of the feet has ranged from natural disasters, including a 2004 tsunami, to drug dealers, serial killers and human traffickers. Another theory is that at least some of the feet came from a 2005 plane crash off Quadra Island. Five men were onboard, but only one of the bodies was found. Others posit that the coast is being used as a dumping ground for victims of organized crime.

According to scientists who analyzed the feet, they were likely detached from bodies due to the push and pull of turbulent waves. Further, several of the feet have been identified as belonging to individuals who suffered from depression, other forms of mental illness and/or had been reported missing. The King County Medical Examiner's Office in Washington indicated that these individuals may have committed suicide by jumping off local bridges, into the water; this could explain why there have been many corpses found floating around these waters. Detached feet were found most recently in 2019.

There are no absolute answers, and the mystery continues. One thing is clear—these events truly make the area a "graveyard" of the Pacific.

Disaster of the Sidewheeler *Pacific*

The loss of the sidewheeler *Pacific* may well have been the worst shipwreck in Pacific Coast history, with perhaps as many as five hundred lives lost.

The *Pacific* was built in 1850 in New York City. It weighed 876 tons, was wooden hulled and 223 feet long, with a width of 33 feet. On its maiden voyage, it broke the one-day speed record for passage down the East Coast. By the early 1870s, it was well past its prime, and in 1872, the ship was left to rot in the "boneyards" on the mudflats near San Francisco. But the 1874–76 gold rush demanded ships to sail the Pacific, and the ancient *Pacific* was hauled from the mudflats. It was given a cosmetic makeover, costing $40,000. The *Pacific* was inspected and described as "fine and sound." But the men who had worked on it reported that its waterlogged wood was so rotten it could be scooped out with a shovel. Also, as work began on the ship, dozens of rats ran off—an unlucky seafaring sign.

It was Thursday, November 4, 1875, when the *Pacific* left Victoria, BC, Canada. It made a stop in Tacoma, Washington, on its way to San Francisco, California. The ship was so packed with passengers, its cabin and dormitory areas were filled beyond capacity; passengers were bedded down in the saloon, and others slept on deck. The best-known passengers aboard were Dennis Kane and Richard Lyon, who discovered the Cassiar goldfields and incited the rush to Northwestern BC. Cassiar later became a ghost town. Also onboard were numerous unnamed miners who swarmed aboard the ship at the last minute, presumably in a hurry to return south before the Canadian winter. The *Pacific* carried a large cargo of food supplies, sundries, hides, buggies, horses and cash.

At thirty-four years old, Captain Jefferson Davis "J.D." Howell was in charge of the *Pacific*'s final voyage. He was the younger brother of Varina Howell Davis, the first lady of the Civil War–era Confederate States of America. Captain Howell was reputedly an inept, inexperienced and incapable master. It was also said that he was intoxicated at the time of the disaster. However, Captain Howell was educated at the U.S. Naval Academy in Annapolis, Maryland, and had, in fact, spent a great deal of time at sea; the *Pacific* was not his first command. Further, passenger Henry Jelly, one of the only two survivors, indicated that Captain Howell was not intoxicated.

There is no doubt that the passengers hurried indoors as quickly as possible when the *Pacific* departed under dark skies and deteriorating weather. It was reported that the morning of the *Pacific*'s departure, the sky glowed an odd red color. Could storms and rough seas have been ahead? The rotten vessel barely made headway. Witnesses on other ships in the harbor described the *Pacific* as making awkward progress and tilting to one side. Henry Jelly testified that Captain Howell inexplicably ordered all of the lifeboats along one side of the ship to be filled with water to act as counterbalance, counteracting the tilting. This seemingly sealed the fate of the many souls on board. One could argue that Howell did the best he could as the commander of a single-deck, nine-hundred-ton vessel with over five hundred people crammed aboard, showing stability problems and sailing into a mounting gale. To his credit, Howell corrected the tilt, but this did not change the ship's unfortunate end.

Interestingly, although the *Pacific* was scheduled to arrive and depart from Tacoma the same day, it was delayed until the next day, Friday, after Captain Howell suffered a severe headache and retired to his berth to sleep. Some say this Friday departure further doomed the *Pacific*.

Around 10:00 p.m., while it was just twelve to fifteen miles off the Washington Coast, rounding Cape Flattery, the limping *Pacific* collided with the sailing ship *Orpheus*, which was under the command of Captain Charles Sawyer. The *Orpheus* was northbound out of San Francisco. It was, by all accounts, not a major collision. The *Orpheus* lost some of its rigging, and a section of railing was carried away. Captain Sawyer of the *Orpheus*, fearing that the collision might have damaged the side of his ship, resumed sailing to make shore and assess the damages. The *Pacific* was last seen from aboard the *Orpheus*. The *Pacific* had altered course and was following the *Orpheus* toward the shore.

Despite the light impact, the *Pacific* began breaking up soon after the collision. Bedlam pursued, and with no one seemingly at the helm, the wind and waves steered the ship. Many of the lifeboats had so much water in them, they were unusable. At least one lifeboat was lowered and swamped during the *Pacific*'s brief remaining time afloat. Other boats were jammed with passengers and crew but could not be put over the rail, and some ten minutes after the accident, the *Pacific* broke into two or three sections, with its funnel collapsing on survivors in the water. It sank in the frigid waters.

Perhaps twenty survivors made it to rafts and floating debris, but over the next day, all but two either succumbed to hypothermia from the frigid waters or were swept off by the waves. One of those lost included Captain Howell, who clung to a section of the hurricane deck with the larger of the two groups of survivors who came together in the water. Henry F. Jelly, who first clung to the overturned lifeboat, then a hen coop and, finally, the roof of the *Pacific*'s pilothouse, was found by accident by the *Messenger* a day and a half after the disaster. His tale of the *Pacific* rolling onto its side and breaking apart and the panic of passengers and crew was initially met with some skepticism.

Of the more than five hundred passengers and crew members, two men, Jelly and Quartermaster Neil O. Henley, survived. Scottish-born Henley was found nearly three days after the sinking by the U.S. Coast Guard revenue cutter and search vessel *Oliver Wolcott*. His story reinforced that of Mr. Jelly in most ways. Henley outlived the *Pacific* by some sixty-nine years, dying in Steilacoom, Washington, on March 14, 1944. Henry Jelly died in Canada in 1930.

Fragments of the *Pacific*, including a portion of its bow that apparently snapped off during the collision and became entangled in the *Orpheus*'s rigging, were widely scattered along the Washington Coast. They were reportedly so rotten that they could be picked apart by one's fingers. A few bodies, perhaps as many as twenty, were recovered, but the majority of those who went down with the *Pacific* were lost at sea forever. The American investigation, held in San Francisco, was widely considered a whitewash. It was held behind closed doors and concluded that the *Orpheus* bore most of the blame for the disaster. Further, it was said that the *Pacific* did not sink because it was rotten, per se, but because of a chance meeting between a lightweight steamship hull that would have crumbled when brand new and that of a staunch sailing vessel. Following the collision, the *Orpheus* attempted to sail to Vancouver Island in Canada but ran aground on Tzartus Island. There were no casualties, and the *Oliver Wolcott* rescued the passengers and crew.

The disaster had a regional impact similar to that of the much later sinking of the *Titanic* in 1912. It remained in the public's memory for some time after its loss. One partially fictionalized account of the *Pacific*'s departure, written thirty years after the sailing by a newspaper editor who witnessed the departure from the dock, described at least five hundred passengers on the doomed ship. One of these passengers he identified as Fannie Palmer, a young, popular member of Victorian society who was surrounded by well-wishers as she prepared to depart for San Francisco. Palmer bid farewell to her friends, fatalistically mentioning that she felt she was seeing them for the last time. Those on the wharf gave three rousing cheers as the ship departed. The writer saw Mrs. Digby Palmer standing on the dock, who exclaimed that she was seeing the last of Fannie. In fact, Fannie was killed in the shipwreck, her body carried forty miles by the tide to the San Juan Island Beach, almost within sight of the family's house. She was buried in a ceremony that was attended by hundreds. The writer also said the disaster resulted in dozens of families being destroyed and two suicides in San Francisco. He told of seeing a small, sweet-faced, blue-eyed boy onboard the ship as it sailed. The editor was tortured for years to come by the images of Fannie Palmer and the small boy.

As the years progressed, only a few old-timers along the Pacific Coast could remember the awful tale of the *Pacific*. This event was ripe for something experienced in other, similar disasters—a ghost ship. In such cases, the specter of the doomed ship is sometimes seen at the site where it went down. It appears without warning, seemingly coming out of nowhere or suddenly exiting a fog bank, usually at dusk or dawn. Such a ship would be gray with age and, in this case, list to one side. It would display no lights, make no sound or waves and leave no wake. One could expect to see the spirits of Fannie Palmer and the small boy onboard the spectral *Pacific*. There is no doubt that these ghosts would be lamenting their sorry fate. There would be whispers and moans of distress carried by the wind. There would be an overwhelming blast of putrid, sea-drenched air as it passes. The ship, as is reported in other cases of ghost ships, would relive its last moments, but this time, it would narrowly miss the collision that sealed its fate. Finally, it would disappear back into the fog.

If you see such a site, hear disembodied voices or experience such an unexplainable event, you may be facing the ghosts of the doomed sidewheeler *Pacific*.

20
VICTORIA AND VANCOUVER ISLAND, BRITISH COLUMBIA, CANADA

ROYAL RUMBLINGS

T he Coast Salish Natives or "First Nations" people, including the Songhees, lived on Vancouver Island for centuries before the Europeans arrived. The Canadian city of Victoria, named for Great Britain's then-queen, is one of the oldest cities in the Pacific Northwest. Formed in 1843 as a Hudson's Bay Company trading post, it became a boomtown in 1858; following the discovery of gold, its population grew from three hundred to five thousand. Victoria became an incorporated city in 1862. As the capital of BC, Victoria is a lovely, historic waterfront city. Despite its serene nature, locals claim Victoria is one of the most haunted cities in Canada.

THE "SCREAMING DOPPELGANGER"

There are stories of numerous suicides, accidents and other fatalities occurring at Victoria's Beacon Hill Park. In one case, at an outcropping of rocks in the park, close to St. Ann's Academy, a woman's murdered body was reportedly found. In life, the woman's friends said they once saw her at the same spot where her body was found, with her arms outstretched, looking at the sky. The woman reportedly denied ever doing this. While her murder was never solved, witnesses have described seeing her ghost or doppelganger at sunrise, standing on top of the same rocks, looking to the sky with her arms outstretched and appearing to scream.

Photograph of Victoria, Canada statue, 2013. *Courtesy of Keithjj, Pixabay.*

BASTION SQUARE PHANTOMS

The most haunted place in Victoria is thought to be Bastion Square, located in the heart of Victoria's Old Town. Hangings were commonplace there in the mid-1800s. Formerly known as Fort Victoria, this part of town was once the site of a jail that housed prisoners on their way to be hanged. They passed through Helmcken Alley on their way to the square.

The spirits of these prisoners and others are said to be abundant there. One spirit is believed to be that of a prisoner who, in the 1850s, was beaten to death by a prison guard. Visitors have reported being followed by the ghost of a man in chains, as well as hearing the sound of chains rattling. Next to the alley, in the basement of the Rithet Building, is the site of Fort Victoria's old well. It's said that a First Nations boy slipped and fell to his death in this well. Following the renovation of the site in 1978, the boy's spirit has been seen walking around and playing in the lobby of the Rithet Building before vanishing back into the well, which still exists in the rear of the building.

The popular Garrick's Head Pub, one of the oldest English pubs in Canada, is said to be the place where prisoners who were heading to the gallows had their last meal. The ghost of one-time pub owner Mike Powers is said to haunt this site; he was murdered over one hundred years ago. It is said that his ghost can be seen by the fireplace on cold nights.

Finally, the site formerly known as "Camille's Restaurant," also in Bastion Square, is reportedly haunted. Legend has it that a man named Brady was waiting for his companion Charlotte at the restaurant, where they frequently dined. Brady got into a fight, a bottle was smashed over his head, his throat was slashed, he staggered out of the pub and soon died. It is believed Brady and Charlotte still visit the restaurant, with visitors reporting the unexplainable scent of heavy cigar smoke and plentiful perfume.

SPECTRAL THEATERS

The elegant, Baroque Revival–style 104-year-old downtown McPherson Playhouse, built in 1914, is said to be the site of a great deal of paranormal activity. One resident spirit is said to be the "Grey Lady." She is described as kind and benign but unsettling. Her spirit was last seen in the late 1990s, during a dress rehearsal for the play *A Woman in Black*. Actors complained of a mysterious woman in the balcony, despite the theater being locked to all but the actors. The theater has been unable to keep an overnight janitor employed due to the lady's presence. It also keeps "ghost lights" lit continuously to keep the spirits at bay.

The classical and elegant Royal Theater, built in 1913, is thought to be home to the ghostly apparition of a man. Visitors and event attendees have reported experiencing the feeling of being "stabbed" by an unseen force.

HAUNTED CEMETERIES

Victoria's "Old Burying Ground" is now known as Pioneer Square. It served as a cemetery from 1855 to 1873, and still holds 1,300 bodies. The site was turned into a park in 1908, after the stone monuments were removed. The community is said to have been up in arms over this, and the park manager resigned. The spirits of those buried there are said to wander the former cemetery.

The first cemetery ghost sighting is believed to have occurred on Christmas Eve in 1861. The ghost was said to have been that of Adelaide Griffin, and it was called "the White Lady of Langley Street." As the story goes, Adelaide, who was in her thirties, and her husband, Ben, relocated from San Francisco and opened the Boomerang Inn and Saloon, located across the street from the old jail yard, in the 1850s. Reportedly, whenever a hanging took place, the Griffins did excellent business. Suddenly and without explanation, Adelaide died. She was buried in the Old Burying Ground. Ever since, her spirit has been seen on Christmas Eve at the site of the old Boomerang Saloon in Pioneer Square.

Another observed ghost is said to be that of Robert or Richard Johnson. In the 1870s, Johnson slit his own throat, committing suicide across the street from Pioneer Square. His spirit can reportedly be seen reenacting his suicide.

Victoria's Ross Bay Cemetery is said to be home to several roaming spirits. In a well-known, 1890 Christmas Eve political murder in Victoria, twenty-eight-year-old David Fee was shot to death as he left the St. Andrews Cathedral. The shooting occurred during the midnight mass, and worshippers found Fee's body lying lifeless on the Cathedral's steps; he was on his way to a Christmas party. In a driving rainstorm, the Cathedral worshippers carried Fee's body to the location of the Christmas party. Fee was found dressed in a white raincoat with a child's toy trumpet hanging around his neck.

The *Daily Colonist* newspaper described Fee's death as "a crime as dark, cowardly and mysterious as ever disfigured the history of this province." The murderer, Lawrence Phelan, surrendered just after the murder, telling a constable, "I am the man that shot a man tonight." As it turned out, Phelan had mistakenly believed that Fee was Thomas Deasy, who was known for his white raincoat. Phelan intended to murder Deasy because he had ordered a political flag advocating Irish independence from Great Britain be taken down. Phelan was sentenced to life in prison but served only ten years.

Fee's body was buried at Ross Bay Cemetery, his grave marked with a huge marble pillar. His bloodied, white-coated ghost has been seen haunting his tomb and the steps of St. Andrews.

Other Ross Bay Cemetery apparitions that have been seen include that of Isabella Ross, the first woman to own land in the province. Her farm stood where the cemetery is now. The ghosts of an elderly couple dressed in formal Victorian attire have also reportedly been seen in the late evening, gliding together along the western side of the cemetery.

PARLIAMENT BUILDINGS PHANTOM

The parliament buildings in Victoria are said to be haunted by the spirit of their famous architect, who also designed Victoria's Empress Hotel: Francis Rattenbury of Great Britain. It is said that both he and his young second wife, Alma, had scandalous affairs. Alma's teenage lover, chauffer George Stoner, admitted to murdering Rattenbury in Bournemouth, England, in 1935 while under the influence of cocaine. Francis Rattenbury's head was caved in by multiple blows from a carpenter's mallet.

Though Stoner was convicted of the murder, Alma was acquitted of any involvement. When she left the Old Bailey Courthouse, she was booed by the crowds that waited outside. Days later, Alma stabbed herself in the heart six times before falling into a river, dead. The sensational story of sex, drugs, betrayal, murder and suicide have inspired books, stage plays and television programs. Rattenbury's spirit, said to be a ghostly, thin man with a mustache, has reportedly been seen walking with a cane through both Victoria's parliament buildings and the Empress Hotel.

EMPRESS HOTEL HAUNTS

The Empress Hotel is a landmark, elegant and historical structure. As mentioned, the spirit of its architect, Francis Rattenbury, is said to haunt the hotel. Other reported spirits there include that of an elderly woman who knocks on doors, seemingly looking for someone to help her to her room. Unfortunately, it's said that her room was removed to make space for the elevator. At one time, the Empress Hotel was known to rent its rooms for long-term accommodation, including to the elderly.

During the 1960s, a construction worker reported seeing a shadowy figure swinging from the ceiling inside the Empress Hotel. On researching a possible explanation, he found that a year earlier, another worker had hanged himself in that same location.

CHINATOWN POLTERGEIST

Victoria's Chinatown is the oldest Chinatown in Canada and the second oldest in the world, just after San Francisco's. Fan Tan Alley in Chinatown is

Right: Photograph of the Victoria, Canada Parliament Building. *Public domain*.

Below: Photograph of Victoria, Canada's Chinatown, 2015. *Courtesy of Victoria-Kenny, Pixabay*.

home to the "Gate of Harmonious Interest." Standing thirty-eight feet high, the gate was built in 1981 to scare away evil spirits. The alley was once the center of Victoria's opium dens and gambling rooms. Locals tell of a young Chinese man named Chan who fell in love with a prostitute named Yo Gum and asked her to marry him. She declined, and he, out of jealousy, murdered her with a cleaver. Chan was chased down the Fan Tan Alley and caught by twenty men. Chan later committed suicide by hanging himself. Locals and visitors report seeing his ghost in the form of a shadowy form running through the alley, pushing them against the walls before disappearing.

CASTLE SPIRITS

Victoria is home to several famous and, some say, haunted castles. These include the national historic site Craigdarroch Castle, described as the "quintessential Victorian experience." Built in the late 1800s, Craigdarroch Castle previously served as a military hospital, a college, government offices and a music conservatory. Visitors have reported hearing whispering, a child's crying and a piano playing on its own, as well as seeing objects flying and ghostly candles burning. One spirit is said to be that of Joan, the wife of the original owner and coal baron Robert Dunsmuir.

Built in 1908, Hatley Castle is another lovely national historic site. It was home to Lieutenant Governor James Dunsmuir and his wife, Laura. The castle was later turned into a naval military academy. The first ghost reported at Hatley Castle was that of the Dunsmuir's twenty-one-year-old son, Jim Jr., who had died on his way to fight in World War I as a passenger of the RMS *Lusitania* off the coast of Ireland when it was torpedoed by a German submarine. His body was never found. Academy cadets have reported being dragged out of bed by the ghost of a woman, thought to be Laura, trying to prevent another young man from going to war. The apparition of the Dunsmuir's servant Annabelle has also reportedly been seen by the third-floor window, where she committed suicide after being jilted by her lover.

DOCKYARD OF THE DAMNED AND THE STEAMER *VALENCIA*'S GHOST SHIP

Though Vancouver Island is in Canada, not America, it is part of the Graveyard of the Pacific. And it's said to be haunted. Like elsewhere in the graveyard, barges, barks, clippers, ferries, freighters, schooners and warships have all been lost in the waters off Vancouver Island.

It is said that the remains of a wrecked ship that once traveled the waters of the Pacific Coast can be found in every nautical mile along the craggy shoreline, hidden beneath the waves. Like many of the wrecked ships in the graveyard, these vessels were lost in unrelenting storms, violent waves and for reasons which can't be explained. One ship in particular, the passenger steamer *Valencia*, met its demise in 1906. It has been called the "local *Titanic*," and as many as 181 souls were lost.

The *Valencia* was criticized for being too slow, too small and too open to the elements. It was designated a "second class vessel" and used as a

Artist's rendering of a shipwreck, 2018. *Courtesy of Pixel2013, Pixabay.*

backup, but mostly, it stayed in "moth balls" or storage in San Francisco. In 1906, just ninety days before the massive San Francisco earthquake, it was pressed into service for another ship that was undergoing repairs, and soon, it left San Francisco. Though the *Valencia* and its crew may have avoided the earthquake's wrath, they couldn't avoid that of the Graveyard of the Pacific.

The *Valencia* began its voyage to Seattle on January 20, 1906, with nine officers, fifty-six crew members and at least 108 passengers. The weather deteriorated as strong winds and poor visibility engulfed the ship. Unable to use the stars for navigation, the *Valencia* relied on dead reckoning—an early tool of navigation, in which you calculate your position based on estimated speed and time from a previously determined position—to identify its position. But Captain Johnston did not account for the strong northerly current that sometimes caused ships to overrun the Juan de Fuca Strait, a body of water about ninety-six miles long that serves as inlet from and outlet to the Pacific Ocean. The boundary between Canada and the United States runs down the middle of the strait.

Blinded by the heavy weather, which included icy rain and strong winds, and navigating by dead reckoning in the strong currents, the captain turned the *Valencia* toward the coast. Unfortunately, he missed the entrance to the Juan de Fuca Strait. Just before midnight on January 22, 1906, the *Valencia* struck a rock, like the *Titanic* struck an iceberg, near Pachena Point, rupturing the hull. Thinking that the damage doomed the ship to sinking, the captain ordered it to be beached. Instead, the *Valencia* became stuck on a reef.

The unfolding disaster consisted of several smaller tragedies that were experienced by both the passengers and crew. The ship's crew, purportedly against the captain's orders, attempted to launch lifeboats. Three flipped over on their descent to the water, spilling souls into the water and to their deaths. Three others capsized after reaching the water, and at least one disappeared beneath the waves. For two days, passengers and crew attempted to escape death. A handful of men made it to shore, which was only 330 feet away, but they then faced a sheer cliff. Two of these men sheltered in a cave, only to be chased out of their refuge by the rising tide. The two men then fell to their deaths. The remaining men made it to the Cape Beale Lighthouse, whose keeper called for help by telegraph. The tug *Salvor* and the vessels *Queen* and *City of Topeka* rushed to the scene but to no avail. Captain Ernest Jordan of the *Salvor* was kept at bay by the giant waves battering the *Valencia*. He expressed frustration at not being able to attempt a rescue as he watched the wreck break up and saw individuals dropping into the "boiling sea."

Soaked, shivering and terrified, men, women and children clung to the rigging as the *Valencia* broke apart. The last of the passengers and crew were sent to their deaths by drowning, exposure and pounding against the rocks. As many as 181 lives were lost, including all of the women and children. Only 37 men survived the shipwreck. The inquiry that followed the wreck found that the launching orders for the lifeboats were poorly timed and that the crew had not been properly trained and drilled.

The loss of the *Valencia* horrified the people of Victoria, Canada. Canada responded to the disaster by constructing a lighthouse and regularly spaced shelters with lifesaving supplies maintained inside. The Pachena Point Lighthouse was finished in 1908, and in 1911, the series of shelters were completed.

As is often the case with shipping disasters in the graveyard, the story of the *Valencia*—as a ghost ship—continues.

The ship's cook, a veteran of four other shipwrecks, is said to have felt an unnatural foreboding before the *Valencia*'s departure. His last words as he went down with the ship are now legendary: "I should have known all along that she was doomed!" Sailors have reported seeing a strange steamer working the coastline near the wreck, years after the tragedy. They said the vessel "resembled the ill-fated *Valencia*" and that they "could vaguely see human forms clinging to her mast and rigging." In addition, ghostly lifeboats have been spotted rowing through the surf.

Photograph of a wrecked boat. *Courtesy of Pixabay.*

In 1933, twenty-seven years after the wreck, the *Valencia*'s lifeboat no. 5 came ashore in Barkley Sound. The boat was inexplicably in good condition, with much of its original paint intact and the boat's nameplate still fastened to its side. These reinforced the stories of a haunted ghost ship.

Could it be that Vancouver Island's "Dockyard of the Damned," so named due to the *Valencia* and many ships wrecked in nearby waters, is haunted with the spirits of doomed sailors and passengers? This watery graveyard tale is similar to others we've discussed, and such a haunting could be easily conjectured. Given the remote location of the sinking of the *Valencia*, its remains have been left relatively untouched and remain along the coast.

21
PUGET SOUND AND SEATTLE, WASHINGTON

PHANTOM FINISH

The Puget Sound, an inlet of the Pacific Ocean along the northwest coast of Washington State, and Seattle area are beautiful seafaring areas with a great deal of history. In 1792, explorer George Vancouver named the area in honor of his accompanying lieutenant Peter Puget. The area was home to numerous Native tribes, including the Duwamish, Samish, Sammamish, Skokomish, Skykomish, Snohomish and Stillaguamish. The ending "ish" in each of the tribes' names means "people of." White settlers who arrived along the Oregon Trail settled the area, and like many of the areas we have explored, tales of hauntings are abundant there.

PORT TOWNSEND HAUNTINGS

Port Townsend is a lovely Victorian seaport with a rich history. Twisted History Tours, a paranormal investigation company, says the town is one of the top-twenty most haunted locations in the United States.

Described by many as "colorful," Captain Henry Tibbals arrived in the Puget Sound area in 1856, after serving as the master of several sailing vessels. He established several hotels—the Palace, the Pioneer and the Union Wharf. The beautiful Victorian Palace Hotel, located in the Captain Henry Tibbals building (constructed in 1889) originally housed a billiard parlor and saloon called the Townsend Tavern on the lower floor.

Photograph of a Native totem pole, 2019. *Courtesy of Abhardphoto, Pixabay.*

From 1925 to 1933, the top two floors of the Palace were nicknamed "the Palace of Sweets," as it served as both a brothel and hotel. Rooms were named for "working girls," including the "Madame Marie's Suite" and the "Miss Kitty's Room." Marie is said to have occupied the corner suite on the second floor, Room 4. Her room was richly decorated with red wallpaper and green wood trim, and it housed the only fireplace in the building. The local sheriff raided the brothel in the mid-1930s, forcing the brothel to close. Beginning in the 1940s, another female spirit has been observed walking through the halls of the second floor. This ghost is said to be that of Miss Genevieve, one of the former "ladies of the night," whose portrait, called the *Lady in Blue*, hangs in the hotel at the top of the stairs. Moving and falling objects, strange shadows, levitating beds and unexplained sounds have been detected, as have reports of ladders being knocked out from under workers. Some staff reportedly refuse to work on the third floor for fear of coming into contact with a ghost.

The lovely Victorian Ann Starrett Mansion was similarly built in 1889. It is said to be haunted by its former owners George and Ann Starrett. Also believed to be present is the red-haired ghost of the Starrett's child's nanny. Pictures fall, lights turn off, radios play static and guests have reported being touched on the head when the nanny's spirit passes. A women's group that met in the mansion reportedly observed a female spirit floating down the stairs.

The 1892 Greek Revival Manresa Castle has served as a private home, a Jesuit college and a hotel. It is reputedly haunted by two specters, believed to be those of a priest who hanged himself in Room 302 and a woman who jumped from the window of Room 306. The woman is said to have been distraught over a lover who never returned from the sea. Hotel guests have reported being touched while sleeping and seeing swaying light fixtures, ghostly orbs and mist, as well as hearing unexplained thumping noises. In the 1970s, a hotel housekeeper reported seeing his keys, which he had set down on a table in room 306, floating in midair, about eighteen inches above the table, before they crashed back down.

PORT ANGELES' GHOSTLY UNDERGROUND

The historic waterfront town of Port Angeles is known by many as the "jumping off" point for ferries that are heading to and from Victoria, Canada. It also has an underground that was created in 1914, when the town's streets were raised fourteen feet above the sewage-strewn tidal flats. Due to flooding concerns at the time, Port Angeles elevated its downtown streets, creating underground tunnels and storefronts. What had formerly been the first floors of waterfront buildings were turned into basements. The underground is home to old store fronts and is said to be haunted.

The oldest remaining building in Port Angeles was built in 1913. The building was reportedly home to bootleggers who illegally produced and sold liquor in the 1920s and early 1930s, during Prohibition. The second floor of the building was a brothel until 1942. Paranormal investigators visited the area in the summer of 2009 and photographed what they described to be faces staring out of windows in the underground. Halloween events and tours are held annually in the Port Angeles underground, giving insight into the living history of the town.

SPOOKY SEATTLE

We began our road trip with one of the largest cities we visited: Portland, Oregon. We will now finish our journey with the largest city discussed in this book: Seattle, Washington, where haunted locations abound in this beautiful setting.

In 1851, settlers first called the area "New York" but later changed it to Seattle in honor of Duwamish and Suquamish Native leader Chief Seattle (1786–1866), who had befriended the settlers. Seattle is nicknamed the "Emerald City," as the city itself and the surrounding areas are filled

Photograph of Seattle, Washington, 1898–1931. *Courtesy of the Miriam and Ira D. Wallach Photography Collection, New York Public Library.*

with greenery year-round. In the 1850s, Seattle produced lumber for San Francisco and towns in the Puget Sound area. In the 1870s, coal was discovered near Lake Washington, and the Northern Pacific Railway Company announced that it would build its westernmost point in Tacoma, forty miles south of Seattle. Northern Washington State, from Tacoma to Seattle, and the Puget Sound boomed, with logging, coal, fishing, trade and shipbuilding as the leading industries. By the 1890s, Seattle was gaining about one thousand residents every month.

HAUNTED UNDERGROUND

Below historic Pioneer Square, Seattle's original neighborhood, are tunnels that once comprised downtown Seattle. Downtown Seattle was built at sea level and was prone to flooding and sewage problems. The great Seattle fire of June 6, 1889, which started when glue boiled over and ignited wood chips in a carpentry shop, devastated much of the former downtown area. The city was rebuilt, raising the street level two stories and creating a labyrinth of underground storefronts and tunnels. The underground continued to be used for business purposes before closing in 1907. Illegal activities, including opium dens and brothels, were reportedly present there until the 1940s, when the underground was abandoned. The underground is now used primarily for ghost tours.

A ghost named Edward reportedly resides in the underground. He is said to have a handlebar moustache, wears suspenders and is believed to have possibly been a bank teller who was shot and killed during the Klondike Gold

Rush of the late 1890s. Another ghost is said to be that of a woman who was murdered and placed behind a bank vault (there's no other information related to this case). In addition to the sightings of ghostly figures, cold spots and floating orbs have been observed by those visiting the underground. A fictitious version of the Seattle underground was used as the haunted setting for the 1973 television horror and mystery movie *The Night Strangler*, a film about a serial killer who used his victims' blood to keep himself alive for over a century. The movie has become a "cult" classic and motivated more-recent television programs, including *The X-Files*. It offers a fascinating glimpse into the history behind Seattle's original downtown, which is now underground.

SORRENTO HOTEL SPECTERS

The most haunted location in Seattle is said to be the upscale, lavish Sorrento Hotel. *USA Today* named the Sorrento one of the country's thirteen most haunted hotels in 2015. Built in 1909, this luxurious destination is reportedly home to the ghost of marijuana activist Alice B. Toklas, who was also the longtime partner of famed writer Gertrude Stein. Toklas was born in San Francisco in 1877 and moved to Seattle in 1890. In 1900, she returned to San Francisco. After surviving the 1906 San Francisco earthquake, in 1907, Toklas moved to Paris, where she met Stein, and she died there in 1967. Hotel staff have reported seeing Toklas's spirit, dressed in either a white or black shroud, in Room 408, as well as floating down hallways while lights

Photograph of Seattle, Washington. *Courtesy of Pixabay.*

flicker. In an October 2019 article titled "5 Haunts with Haunts," the *New York Times* identified Room 408 as Toklas's regular accommodation. Drinks in the hotel's Dunbar Room have been said to move as her spirit passes, and a cocktail has been named in her honor.

KELLS' KREEPERS

Kells Irish Restaurant and Pub is described as having great food and drink. It has also been called America's most haunted pub and was featured on a 2010 episode of the Travel Channel's *Ghost Adventures*. Originally known as Seattle's Butterworth Building when it was built in the early 1900s, the location was used by Butterworth & Sons Mortuary for the city's victims of a diphtheria epidemic, poor sanitation, mining accidents and violence. The building is in the National Register of Historic Places and housed the first elevator on the West Coast, which was used to transport bodies. The mortuary contained a thirty-five-coffin showroom, with coffins for both children and adults, priced from $25 to $200. Women's burial garments were also sold, costing from $4 for a robe to $125 for fancier clothing. There were private rooms for those who wished to have a final visit with their loved one's remains. It is said that bodies arrived through the same door that visitors now use to enter the bar.

A ghost named Charlie has been reported to look at guests through a mirror, and the spirit of a little girl has been seen sitting near the bar, trying to get the children who are visiting the restaurant to play with her. Glasses have been observed sliding onto the floor on their own, mirrors have mysteriously shattered, plaster has fallen randomly from the walls and ceiling and disembodied footsteps and mysterious whispers have been heard.

HIGH SCHOOL APPARITIONS

Since 1920, West Seattle High School has been continuously open and educating students. In 1924, a student named Rose Higginbotham reportedly (no historical documents confirm this) hanged herself at the school. Her spirit is said to roam the halls and has been seen mingling with ghostly "friends" from the same era at the nearby Olmstead Legacy Park at sunrise (or sunset if there is heavy fog or overcast skies). Although no records have been found to confirm Rose's tale, the story persists.

Olmstead Legacy Park is believed to be haunted. The ghosts of Rose and her spirit friends have been seen, as well as animal apparitions.

PIKE PLACE PHANTOMS

A fun tourist area in Seattle is the Pike Place Market, a farmer's market that opened in 1907 and has been going strong ever since. People from around the world come to visit. But there is reputedly a darker side to the market. It is rumored that the market was built on top of a Native burial ground.

We have discussed, at great length, the ramifications of desecrating Native burial places. Princess Angeline, the daughter and last direct descendant of the great Chief Seattle of the Duwamish and Suquamish tribes, lived in a cabin near what is now Pike Place Market. In 1855, the Duwamish tribe entered the Treaty of Point Elliott, which required them to leave. The princess refused and continued to live in her waterfront cabin, where

Photograph of Seattle, Washington's Pike Place Market, 2015. *Courtesy of Foundry, Pixabay.*

Left: Photograph of Native princess Angeline, 1902. *Courtesy of the New York Public Library.*

Right: Artist's rendering of Seattle, Washington. *Courtesy of the New York Public Library.*

she passed away on May 31, 1896. Visitors have reported seeing her spirit wandering around the market, bent over and walking slowly and painfully, wearing a red handkerchief over her head, a shawl and many layers of clothing, as she was known to do in life.

Another reported spirit is that of Arthur Goodwin, the nephew of the original market developer for whom a library near the market is named. It is said that his ghost's silhouette can often be seen looking out from a window in Goodwin Library. Also witnessed near the market is the spirit of a barber nicknamed the "Fat-Lady Barber," who, in life, would sing lullabies to clients, putting them to sleep, before reportedly robbing them. It is said that she died when the floor shop collapsed. Maintenance workers have reported hearing her singing lullabies while they clean.

Unrestful Cemetery

The Grand Army of the Republic (GAR) Cemetery was established in 1895 by five GAR posts in Seattle as a final resting place for those killed in the Civil War. There are 526 graves and a monument memorializing the Civil War soldiers buried here. The GAR posts maintained the cemetery until it was turned over to the City of Seattle in 1922. In the following decades, visitors to the cemetery described it as falling into disrepair until the "Friends of the GAR," an all-volunteer group, was formed in 1996 and took over its care.

The cemetery is believed to be haunted by the ghosts of the dead soldiers buried here. According to witnesses, unexplainable blood-curdling screams and cries can often be heard.

Mortuary Massacre

Appropriately, our last stop is (if it's to be believed) one of the strangest. The Georgetown Morgue is a modern-day haunted house, but there is said to be a real haunted history attached to this facility.

First called Kolling Mortuary Services of Seattle in 1928, the house became Broughton Brothers Funeral Services in 1939. The reported strange events began in 1947, when jazz trumpeter John "Figgy" Dorsey's body, while being prepared for burial, disappeared from the embalming table. His body was said to be found on Mrs. Dorsey's front yard, dismembered. She returned it to Broughton's. In 1965, one of the Broughton brothers, Charles, was reportedly killed when one of the mortuary towers collapsed on him during an earthquake. Charles's widow is thought to have lived in a small house on the west side of the facility until she committed suicide there in 1979.

In the strangest tale attached to this facility, in 1968, the morgue's nine employees were holding a meeting there when two or three armed men came in, bound the workers and placed them in the crematory, where they were burned alive. In 1969, the city acquired the facility and turned it into the Georgetown Morgue, where animal carcasses were processed. Finally, in 1989, the Richland Processing Corporation reportedly bought the morgue and turned it into a meatpacking transport station.

Records of these events are scarce, so we may never know the true story. The facility is purportedly haunted by the spirits of the individuals whose bodies were handled by the morgue and possibly by the employees who were murdered there. If true, this would be similar to other locations we have examined, where the ghosts of individuals who died untimely or dramatic deaths have clung to locations they knew in life.

EPILOGUE

Chilling tales of the paranormal abound in the area known as the Graveyard of the Pacific. From Portland, Oregon, to Seattle, Washington, spirits linger and ghost stories thrive. These spirits are said to be in the waters and weathered communities we have visited.

The graveyard gets its name from the more than two thousand ships and countless lives lost to the treacherous waters; untimely deaths; "shanghaied" sailors and kidnapped women; ghostly tunnels, theaters, castles, brothels, gambling houses and saloons; murderers and their victims; lighthouse keepers' and their families' arduous lives; early settlers' experiences; desecration of Native lands; inappropriate burials and haunted graveyards; legends of buried treasure; stories of Sasquatch; and tales of apparitions, mummies, monsters and werewolves. The graveyard is reported to be home to specters, supernatural beings and unexplainable events.

The dark skies, howling gales, fog and local landmarks colorfully named "Cape Disappointment," "Deadman's Hollow" and "Dismal Nitch" add to the ambience of dread and foreboding.

The legends and tales of hauntings we have explored continue to this day. They serve many purposes: they document paranormal activity, help explain that which is not easily explained and offer a fun escape from reality. Whatever the purpose and whether or not you are a believer, these tales are fascinating and are part of the area's history.

The Graveyard of the Pacific is the most haunted place in America, so please come and visit. Just be careful when you do, as you never know who or what you might run into.

BIBLIOGRAPHY

Alper, Joshua, dir. "Haunted Northwest (documentary)." *Haunted History.* Aired on March 2, 2001, on History Channel.

Becker, Paula. "Columbia River Quarantine Station at Knappton Is Established on May 9, 1899." July 12, 2007. www.historylink.org.

Belyk, R.C. *Great Shipwrecks of the Pacific Coast.* Hoboken, NJ: Wiley, 2001.

Bengel, Eric. "Mary Louise Flavel's Death Closes a Chapter on a Long and Complex History." *Daily Astorian*, November 10, 2018.

Bhattacharjee, S. "7 Most Common Superstitions of Seafarers." *Marine Insight*, 2019.

Blalock, B. *The Oregon Shanghaiers: Columbia River Crimping from Astoria to Portland.* Charleston, SC: The History Press, 2014.

Cemetery Records Online. www.interment.net.

Changler, J.D., and J.B. Fisher. Episode 1. *Portland Unsolved.* Aired in 2018.

City of Portland. "Fire and Rescue." www.portlandoregon.com.

Clearson, C. "Nehalem Tillamook Tales." 1990. www.oregonencyclopedia.com.

Cobb, T. *Ghosts of Portland, Oregon.* Atglen, PA: Schiffer Publishing, 2007.

Cool Interesting Stuff. www.coolinterestingstuff.com.

Daily Colonist, December 25, 1890.

Dalton, A. *The Graveyard of the Pacific: Shipwreck Tales from the Depths of History.* Victoria, BC: Heritage House Publishing, 2020.

Davis, J. *Haunted Tour of the Pacific Northwest.* St. Anthony, NL: Norseman Ventures, 2001.

Deur, Griffin D., and C. La Follette. "The Mountain of a Thousand Holes: Shipwreck Traditions and Treasure Hunting on Oregon's North Coast." Portland State University study, 2018.

Dickey, C. *Ghostland: An American History in Haunted Places*. New York: Viking Press, 2016.

Downer, D.L. *Classic American Ghost Stories: 200 Years of Ghost Lore from the Great Plains, New England, the South and the Pacific Northwest*. Atlanta: August House Publishers, 1990.

Drawson, M.C. *Treasures of the Oregon Country*. N.p.: Dee Publishing Company, 1975.

Duncan-Strong, W. *The Occurrence and Wider Implications of a "Ghost Cult" on the Columbia River Suggested by Carvings in Wood, Bone and Stone*. Whitefish, MT: Literary Licensing LLC, 1945.

Dwyer, J. *Ghost Hunter's Guide to Portland and the Oregon Coast*. New Orleans: Pelican Publishing Company, 2015.

Ferguson-McKeown, M. *The Trail Led North: Mont Hawthorne's Story*. Portland, OR: Binford & Mort Publishers, 1960.

Find a Grave. www.findagrave.com.

Gentling, D. "The Bandage Man Legend: A Cannon Beach Legend." University of Oregon's Northwest Folklore program, 1974.

Ghosts and Gravestones. www.ghostsandgravestones.com.

Ghosts of America. www.ghostsofamerica.com.

Gibbs, J.A. *Pacific Graveyard*. Portland, OR: Binford & Mort Publishing, 1991.

———. *Peril at Sea*. Atglen, PA: Schiffer Publishing Ltd., 1997.

———. *Tillamook Light: A True Account of Oregon's Tillamook Rock Lighthouse*. Portland, OR: Binford & Mort Publishing, 1979.

Gillespie, M.P. *The Myth of an Irish Cinema*. Syracuse, NY: Syracuse University Press, 2009.

Goings, A. *The Port of Missing Men: Billy Gohl, Labor, and Brutal Times in the Pacific Northwest*. Seattle: University of Washington Press, 2020.

Gorrow, Chelsea. "Flavel Family Mystery Unsealed." *Daily Astorian*, July 2, 2012.

Greenman, M. "Haunted Harbor: A Ghost Hunter's Guide to Haunted Places in Grays Harbor County." www.graysharbortalk.com.

Guiley, R.E. "Ghost of a Suicide at Haunted North Head Lighthouse." www.visionaryliving.com.

Hanauer, E. "Seafaring Superstitions & Marine Myth Rituals Explored." August 6, 2006. www.dtmag.com.

Haunted Places. www.hauntedplaces.org.

Hawthorn, T. "Dockyard of the Damned: Vancouver Island's Hidden Shipwrecks." *Globe and Mail-British Columbia*, 2012.

Hellen, Mike. *Oregon's Ghosts & Monsters*. N.p.: Rainy Day Printing, 1983.

Higgins, D.W. *Tales of a Pioneer Journalist: From Gold Rush to Government Street in 19th Century Victoria*. Victoria, BC: Heritage House Publishing Company Ltd., 1996.

Hirschfelder, A., and P. Molin. "The Encyclopedia of Native American Religions, Facts on File." 1992. www.infobaselearning.com.

Historic Tours of America. "Types of Ghosts." www.historictours.com.

Ilwaco Tribune. Obituary for Mary Pesonen. June 1923.

Journal of American Folklore 6 (1893).

Kanuckel, A. "Fata Morgana: The Strange Mirages at Sea." *Farmers' Almanac*, 2021.

Kavanagh, Ivan, dir. *Bandage Man*. 2003.

Kennedy, S. Travel section. *New York Times*, 2006.

Kozik, J. *Shipwrecks of the Pacific Northwest: Tragedies and Legacies of a Perilous Coast*. Guilford, CT: Globe Pequot Press, 2020.

Lansing, R.B. "The Tragedy of Charity Lamb, Oregon's First Convicted Murderess." *Regional Historical Quarterly*, 2000.

Latchana-Kennedy, Karen. *Spine-Tingling Urban Legends*. Minneapolis, MN: Lerner Publishing Group, 2018.

Law Library, American Law and Legal Information. "Charity Lamb Trial, 1854." www.law.jrank.org.

Life Other Than. "The Haunted Historic Tokeland Hotel." www.lifeotherthan.com.

Long, E. "Haunted Peninsula: Our Towns are Alive with Ghosts." *Chinook Observer*, 2005.

Lovecraft, H.P. *The Shadow over Innsmouth*. Scotts Valley, CA: CreateSpace, 2014.

Ludwig, Michaela. "15 Haunted Places in Victoria." *British Columbia Magazine*, October 26, 2015.

Maritime Heritage Project.

McMacken, J. "Spirits Call Port Townsend Home All Year Round." *Peninsula Daily News*, 2017.

Melville, H. *Redburn*. New York: Penguin Random House, 2002.

Miller, M. "Peninsula's History Includes Tales of Ghosts and Apparitions." *Peninsula Daily News*, 2009.

Morton, D.G. 2017, www.hunker.com.

Mrpilikia [pseud.]. "Wreck of the SS *Valencia*: The Remains of the Worst Maritime Disaster in the History of 'Graveyard of the Pacific.'" www.atlasobscura.com.

Oregon. www.oregon.com.

Oregon Coast Beach Connection. www.beachconnection.net.

Oregon Haunted Houses. www.oregonhauntedhouses.com.

Oregonian, December 24, 1885.

———. December 27, 1885.

———. September 9, 1896.

Oregon Journal. "Bunko Kelly Pardoned After Thirteen Years." July 21, 1907.

Oregon Metro. "Block 14 at Lone Fire Cemetery." www.oregonmetro.gov.

"Oregon's Lizzie Borden: Unfaithful, Axe-Wielding Killer, or Mentally Unstable and Abused Wife?" A project of the Department of History at Portland State University, May 7, 2017.

Oregon State Parks. www.stateparks.oregon.gov.

Ostler, J. *Surviving Genocide: Native Nations and United States from the American Revolution to Bleeding Kansas*. London: Yale University Press, 2019.

Portals to Hell. Season 2, episode 4, "The Shanghai Tunnels." Aired in 2020 on Travel Channel.

Rae-McAdams, L. "Things that go Bump on the Coast." *Chinook Observer*, 2012.

"Real-Life 'Twilight' Tribe Has Wolf Connection, Mixed Feelings About Movie." *National Geographic*, 2012.

Reddit. www.reddit.com.

Redfern, N. *The Bigfoot Book: The Encylopedia of Sasquatch, Yeti and Cryptid Primates*. Canton Carter Township, MI: Visible Ink Press, 2015.

Romantic Oregon Coast Vacations website.

Schlosser, S.E. *Spooky Oregon: Tales of Hauntings, Strange Happenings, and Other Local Lore*. Guilford, CT: Globe Pequot Press, 2018.

Seattle Terrors. "Top 10 Most Haunted Places in Seattle." December 27, 2019. www.seattleterrors.com.

Seattle Times, June 1923.

Sharpe, K. "Haunted Houses & Places in Vancouver, Washington." *USA Today*, 2018.

Smith, A.K. "The Legend of Tragedy Graveyard." *Forks Forum*, 2014.

South Bend Journal, June 1923.

State of Washington Department of Archeology and Historic Preservation.

Summers, Ken. "Investigating the Murderous Ghost of William Ghol, the Ghoul of Grays Harbor." February 2, 2015. www.weekinweird.com.

———. "*San Francisco Call*." www.wahauntedhouses.com.

Switzer, S. "Ghost-Dodging in Portland." *National Geographic*, 2012.

Tiffany, Scott, dir. *Lost Secrets*. Season 1, episode 5, "The Lewis and Clark Conspiracy." Aired on December 8, 2019, on Travel Channel.

U.S. government commission. "Wreck of the Steamer Valencia: Report to the President, of the Federal Commission of Investigation," 1906.

U.S. Lighthouses. www.uslighthouses.com.

Wang, KY. "Severed Feet—Still Inside Shoes—Keep Mysteriously Washing up on Pacific Northwest Shores." *Washington Post*, 2016.

Washington's Long Beach Peninsula. "Haunted Places on the Long Beach Peninsula." October 10, 2019. www.visitlongbeachpeninsula.com.

Weaver, F. "Finnish Mythical Creatures Still Lurk." *This Is Finland*, n.d.

Webb, P. "Mary Pesonen 'Walks Again' in Ghost TV Show." *Chinook Observer*, 2018.

Wilma, David. "Graveyard of the Pacific: Shipwrecks on the Washington Coast." September 12, 2006. www.historylink.org.

Wood, M. "The Most Haunted Hotels in the World." *USA Today*, 2014.

Wright, E.W. *Lewis & Dryden's Maritime History of the Pacific Northwest*. N.p.: Lewis & Dryden Printing Co., 1895.

Yuen, C. "The Georgetown Morgue: Gruesome True Story or Fabrication?" *Daily of the University of Washington*, 2008.

Zullo, A. *Tragedy Graveyard, the Starbuck Ghost and Other True Stories*. Mahwah, NJ: Troll Communications, 1996.

ABOUT THE AUTHOR

Ira Wesley Kitmacher is a professor, attorney, speaker, consultant and expert witness. Originally from Massachusetts, he has lived in California, Nevada, Virginia and, now, Washington State. Ira retired in 2019 after serving as a senior federal executive and manager for thirty-six years. He also served as a professor teaching graduate- and undergraduate-level courses for Georgetown University in Washington, D.C.; Portland State University in Oregon; and Grays Harbor College in Aberdeen, Washington.

Ira is fascinated by the history of the American Pacific Northwest, especially the area known as "the Graveyard of the Pacific." He lives in the area with his wife, Wendy; their two children, David and Gabi (when they come to visit); two dogs; and two cats.

He hopes you enjoy this journey through the graveyard as much as he enjoyed writing it!

Visit us at
www.historypress.com